Leadership Lessons-
Straight from the Heart

Leadership Lessons- Straight from the Heart

Turnaround Strategy

Dr M S Phogat

PARTRIDGE
A Penguin Random House Company

Copyright © 2016 by Dr M S Phogat.

ISBN: Softcover   978-1-4828-6876-0
         eBook   978-1-4828-6875-3

All rights reserved. No part of this book may be used or reproduced by any means, graphic, electronic, or mechanical, including photocopying, recording, taping or by any information storage retrieval system without the written permission of the author except in the case of brief quotations embodied in critical articles and reviews.

This is a work of fiction. Names, characters, businesses, professions, places, events and incidents are either the products of the author's imagination or used in a fictitious manner. Any resemblance to actual communities, groups, organizations, institutions, actual person or persons, living or dead, or actual events is purely coincidental. Nor is there any intention whatsoever to denigrate any particular sex, faith, belief, creed and race or hurt any religious sentiments.

Because of the dynamic nature of the Internet, any web addresses or links contained in this book may have changed since publication and may no longer be valid. The views expressed in this work are solely those of the author and do not necessarily reflect the views of the publisher, and the publisher hereby disclaims any responsibility for them.

Print information available on the last page.

To order additional copies of this book, contact
Partridge India
000 800 10062 62
orders.india@partridgepublishing.com

www.partridgepublishing.com/india

Contents

1. Introduction 1
2. Iron Out The Hurdles 18
   a. Removal of Operational Bottlenecks 21
3. Marketing and Publicity 25
   a. Ideas & Constant Change 32
4. Staff Precious Asset 36
5. Search for the Niche 48
   a. Watch for the opportunities 53
6. Managing Profits 59
7. Informality and Flexibility 67
8. Information System and Feed Back 71
9. Proactiveness Passion and Personal Touch 75
10. Visualise the Future Market 84
11. Net Working and Liasoning 89
12. Reporting of Performance 93
13. Increase in Customer Base to Multiply Business 99
14. Involvement 103
15. Handling Critical Issues 106
16. Leadership Defined 122

Chapter 1

Introduction

Points to ponder

- **Do your home work properly**
- **Be confident of achievement**
- **Do SWOT analysis first**
- **Identify the problems**
- **Involve staff in identifying the problems**
- **Get feedback from all concerned**
- **Do not afraid of problems**
- **Find opportunities in challenges**
- **Focus on your strengths first**
- **Search for the niche**
- **Field work is a must**
- **Strong will to find the way**
- **SWOT analysis has the key to solutions**
- **Brain storm in staff meetings**

Chander belonged to a rural family in farming community of Punjab. His father had died when; he was a small child of two years. His mother again married to his uncle. He did not get full love and affection from his parents. He was admitted to school in a small village and studied upto third standard only and started working with his uncle in the farm. One day, he left his home with one of his friend, without any information. These two boys caught a train without ticket and went to Lahore in search of work. While sitting in a park, they met a person who was an agent of the British government to recruit people for the British army. The man asked them, if, they would like to enroll themselves in the army. He would get a commission from their enrolment and give them a part of his commission back. Both of them agreed for the same and went along with the agent. He took them to the officer for recruitment. Their physical and medical test were conducted and ultimately recruited in the army. The agent got his commission and paid to these boys, seven rupees each as agreed by him. They were sent to an army camp and ultimately they had to go for support in the Second World War. They boarded a ship along with some other recruits and left for Italy. Ship went through many countries and they were enjoying a new world. After getting training, he was deployed in medical corps of the Indian army. After five years his uncle came to know that he was in Italy and he started asking him to come back to India. After a lot of pressure from his uncle, he decided to go back to India. He left Italy and came back to India. He again started working with his uncle and doing a job of a loader in the grain market along with transportation of goods by bullock cart. He got married and blessed with four sons and four daughters. They were living in a village of Punjab. Vikram was the eldest son. Chander sold a small piece of land near the city and purchased eleven acres of land in a village which was eight kilometers from the city. Farm land was very fertile and irrigated. Chander started getting good return from the sale of crop and the family started leading a prosperous life. Two elder sister of Vikram could not be sent to school as they had to help their parents in the farm. As, the distance of the farm was approx 8 kilometers from their house, they had to start early morning from their house to reach the farm in time in the morning. Vikram's mother was a very laborious lady. She would wake up at 2.30 am and grind five kg of wheat floor by her hand. Prepare and pack the meal for the family and start for the farm at 4 o clock in the morning. They had a bullock cart and a pair of bullock. Life was very difficult but the family was enjoying it. Land was irrigated from a canal and once in a week, they will have their turn for irrigation for one or two hours, usually in the night. Chander will take clock to see the time of his turn, a lantern, a torch and a spade and move to the farm in the night. There was a big risk of snake bite or wild animals like jackal or fox at night. But still it was being enjoyed.

Some of the other neighbors were also engaged in the same type of work. Chander was more hardworking man than his peers. There will be a lot of work during the ripening of a crop. Entire family had to camp in the farm during at least 25 days. They will prepare their food on the farm and work whole day till late in the evening to remove the grains from the corn. There were no thrashers at that time and the entire process was being done manually with the pair of bullocks, they will reap the crop and make small bundles so that it can dry. Wet plants cannot be put for removal of the grain. After drying the bundles, they will collect entire crop material at one place in a round circle. Pair of bullock will start moving on the crop to crush it. For wheat and gram crop, a roller of stone called Girdi had to be bound with a rope behind a pair of bullock and whole day; it will keep on making rounds on the dry plants with corn. One person had to follow the bullock. It was a very tiring job. During the day, it will be very hot, but the job had to continue for 15- days to properly crush the dried plants so that grains will be removed from it and after that it will be collected together in a heap. Then they will start winnowing. Grain will be separated through natural air by throwing the thrashed plants. One person was needed to use broom to remove straw falling on the grains while fodder will fly away and fall a little away from the grain. Then the grain will be put in the bags for transportation to home. There will be a crop of 100 quintals' of gram and 150 quintals of wheat. After selling it, a good money was made, though the price at that time was very low. When Vikram was hardly six years old, his father planted cotton in their farm. It was to be picked up manually. Once, he accompanied his mother to pick up cotton in the farm. They started early in the morning on foot. Farm was about eight kilometers from their home. Whole day they picked cotton from the field and in the evening again started back on foot. So, it was 16 kilometer journey and whole day moving in the farm for picking cotton. He was so tired that he asked his mother not to grow cotton in future. After some time, his father sold this agriculture land with intention to buy some other land near their village. He could buy only four acres against the earlier land of eleven acres. Some of the sale proceeds of the land were spent on other items and the poverty started showing its results on the family.

Vikram had already started going to school. It was a government primary school. Fees were negligible. After completing primary level, he was admitted to a higher secondary school. It was also a government school and fee was less than one rupee per month. He was a normal student. He was very healthy and his friends used to call him mota i.e. a fat boy. His mother would prepare some good sweet with deshi ghee (local clarified butter) during winter for him to be healthy and strong. He used to play wrestling with the students and usually win from the boys of his age. He was a player of hockey and football as well. When, he was a student of tenth class, he used to do yoga and race for at least one hour in the morning. It kept his health very well. He passed his higher secondary securing only fifty percent marks. His parents were not much concerned about his studies. They were of the opinion that he is doing his studies reasonably well. Financial position of the family was very fragile and many times, he thought to leave his studies and start working. Once, his father gave him an electricity bill of their tube well at the farm which was amounting to rupees eleven and asked him to write an application for disconnection of electricity connection, as, there was no money with them to pay the bill. This incident made lifelong impact on him and he realized their poverty for the first time. During his days at school and college, he used to assist his parents. Just after coming back from college, he will go to their farm and assist his father. He knew, how to repair the diesel engine of their tube well. So, whenever, there was any problem with the engine, he will open its nuts and bolts, bring a spare part from the market and repair it.

After higher secondary, he was admitted to a nearby college. Payment of fee was always a problem. His father will ask one of his relative Mr. Prabhu, who was a driver at Municipal Committee to lend rupees two hundred to pay for the admission fee of Vikram. After selling the crop, the money will be returned without any interest. It was a big relief to his father. In the first year at college, he found that mathematics was a tough subject. There were many students at the college. The college was under Punjab University. Many students used unfair means during the exam and the university took a very tough stand. Many students, who used unfair means, were identified from their answers papers and cases of unfair means were registered against them. They were debarred for three years. Those who did not use unfair means, were given very tough marking and many such students failed. Vikram failed in the first year of his college. It was a big shock to him as well as his parents. Next year, he did a lot of hard work and now the mathematics had become a very interesting subject for him. He stood first in the college. His base had improved a lot and he was the topper of the college, continuously for three years. Apart from studies, he was a very good speaker, member of drama team, music team, hockey team, athletics teams, and Under Officer of National Cadets Corps at his college. He had a big passion to be an army officer. He passed the written test but could not be selected in army/navy/ air force. He along with some of his friends formed an Arya Samaj i.e. a religious group for teaching spiritualism and yoga to students and children of their neighborhood. He was regarded as a very respectful, gentle and well mannered boy.

He passed his graduation with commerce and applied for admission to MBA and Master of Commerce. He could not be selected for MBA but was very high in the merit for admission to M.Com. He thought that regular Masters will be a costly affair and family may not be in a position to afford. He decided to find some job and registered for M. Com from Rajasthan University under distance education. He got a call from employment exchange after two month of passing B.Com for a job of a clerk in irrigation department of the state Government. He was selected at a monthly stipend of rupees two hundred only. He preferred to join the job. After six month, it was to be converted to a regular job with a monthly salary of rupees four hundred. When he got his first stipend of rupees two hundred, he saved rupees fifty and sent a money order to his father. His father was very happy on getting rupees fifty. In the meantime, he applied for the job of a clerk in a bank. Appeared in the test and passed. Interview panel asked him about the working in a farm and various types of manures, which he had been doing with his father. He replied all the questions of the interview panel and the panel was happy with his responses. He got selected as a bank clerk cum cashier. Now, the salary was about six hundred per month. He could repay the debt of his family. He wanted to do something special in his life. He never wanted to be an ordinary employee of the bank. He was very hard working, sincere, obedient and dedicated worker. His manager was very happy with his work. He kept on studying for M. Com and registered as a member of the Indian Institute of Bankers. There were five papers in part one and six papers in part two of the CAIIB, in all, eleven papers for getting the certificate of both parts of

CAIIB. He passed those papers. He also passed the written test for directly recruited officers, but, could not be selected because he could not speak English at the interview and the interview panel members asked him to speak in English only. After four years of his job, he got through in the promotion test and became an officer. He was transferred to Uttar Pradesh in a rural branch. It was a new experience for him. Though, it was a rural branch but very big branch with currency chest facility. There were many sugar mills and rice mills in the area. He was put as the credit officer and his job was to process loan proposals, monitoring and follow up of advances. Several times, he was sent on deputation as branch manager to nearby branches, whenever, some manager will go on leave. After four years of stay at rural areas, he was transferred back to Delhi. After four years of coming back to Delhi, he became eligible for promotion to Managers cadres. He was very focused and hard working, therefore, got through in his first attempt. He was put as a joint Manager along with his duties as a credit officer. It was an additional responsibility. After some time, he was again transferred to another big branch where the credit portfolio was very big. He was again given the credit responsibility as manager credit. He was so sincere and honest that most of the branch managers will request the Regional Manager that Vikram be given to them as credit officer. He changed several branches and became Senior Manager. Apart from his job, he had developed a passion for academics. So, he got himself registered for Ph.D. He got an excellent guide for his Ph.D study who was the Director at the Institute of Management Studies and Research. While, he was doing his Ph.D, he thought that it will be the best, if, he gets an opportunity to work as a training faculty. Bank issued a circular for selection of training faculties and he applied for the position. During the selection process after group discussions, there was a personal interview. Chairman of the panel was impressed by the style and his sense of humor. During the interview itself, he was told that he will be identified for the apex training college of the bank. After some time the letter came and he joined the training system. It was a memorable experience at the staff college as faculty. He was a very passionate faculty. He will spend more time with his participants than that of other faculties. He will call the participant at nine AM in the morning instead of 9.30 AM which was the normal time of classes. There will be learning diary session to repeat the learning of the previous day. He will clarify all the doubts of his participant. After the classes in the evening, he will start working on the topics to be taken on the next day and some times, he will have extra classes on IT matters internet, emails etc. After having prepared for the topics for the next day, he will start working on his Ph.D theses. He had been working till late mid night. Ultimately, he completed and submitted his theses in March 2003 and the degree was awarded in November 2003.

While at the college, he got an opportunity to apply for the overseas posting for working at some branches of the bank in other countries. Bank had a very rigorous process for identification of the people for overseas branches. Now, his storey of working at the overseas territory and its transformation started, which is a very interesting story.

Vikram took over a silent, stagnant and sleeping banking organization and transformed it into a vibrant organization, within a period of two years. People had no knowledge about this bank, despite being in existence for the last 28 years. Public had a perception that it is a bank only for a limited people of Indian origin. Some people thought, it was a Pakistani Bank. There were hardly a few customers seen in the bank and the staff had not much work to do. Staff was doing its routine duty and going home at 4 pm. Motivation and morale of the staff was not very high. Business was showing declining trend for the last several years. Top management was seriously considering the closure of operation of the territory. The country was suffering from externalization problem and the branch was having problems in remittance of past profits. Two loan exposures of very high value had gone bad and it was a very big problem to recover the same. Bank had already lost the legal battle in one of the big loan, where the outstanding was more than USD100 million. It was a big challenge to **steer** the organization successfully with positive results and build the image of the bank as a proactive and vibrant organization.

Before going to that country as the Chief Executive and Territory Head, Vikram had a very good exposure of working as Chief Manager training at Bank's Staff College Ahmedabad, which was the apex institution of training system of the bank. He had completed four years of his tenure of five years as faculty. He had already worked in several branches, mainly as Credit Officer/Manager or Senior Manager Operation, a post of second in command after the branch head. Bank had never given him an opportunity to work as a head of the branch. Therefore, he was denied promotion to the next grade in 2005, as, he had no experience of handling a branch as a Branch

Head. Identification of officers for overseas assignment in the bank was a very rigorous exercise, containing written test, group discussions and personal interview. During the personal interview, one of the panel members, after getting satisfactory replies to all the technical questions, again raised the issue that he had never been a branch head. How can he handle a territory? Chairman of the interview panel, then said that he has not been given an opportunity to be a branch head, let us test him. He was then identified as the Chief Executive and Territory Head of Victoria.

As part of his training for overseas posting, he had to visit their bank's International Division and study the important files and issues related to the territory. He was briefed by the then General Manager (International Operations) that it was a dead territory. There was no business growth. It is a very small country. Do not take long term and big exposures. Bank may need to close the operations of this territory at any time. Vikram replied, if you are sending Vikram, you cannot close the territory, even if, you want it. He was confident that business will grow and he shall get back his business share from the competitors. He studied the files related to the important issues of the territory. All the files related to advances, non performing assets, legal cases, issues pertaining to the Government of the country, HR issues. He also studied about the country, its economy, major business and industrial activities, currency, parity with other currencies and its movements in the past few years, budget, political system, banking system and Central Bank of the country, the regulator of the banks, various acts related to banking and finance, and the latest who is who of banking and the Government. He requested the existing

Chief Executive to give him a brief about the essential commodities, their prices and the things which needed to be brought from India. He planned his journey in the light of the information gathered through various sources.

Ultimately, he landed in the new territory on 23.06.2006 along with his wife. Mr. Goyal, the acting Chief Executive along with the Driver came to receive him at the airport. It was a Saturday and half day working of the bank and he reached at around 2 pm. He asked Mr. Goyal about the staff, whether available in the branch at that time or left for home. Mr. Goyal told him that some staff members were still working in the branch. Mr. Goyal asked him, if he would like to go to branch or home and take rest. Vikram decided to go to the branch directly. He was very happy to see the nice bank branch, very neat and clean. They entered from the staff gate. Vikram wished good afternoon everybody and all the staff members looked happy to see him. He had introduction with all the staff present at the branch and had a round of the branch to have a complete awareness of the branch. His predecessor had already left in October 2005. He took charge from the Second in command Mr. Goyal. The first thing, he discussed with Mr. Goyal was the Strengths Weaknesses, Opportunities and Threats (SWOT) of the bank's operations and some feedback about the staff. Mr. Goyal gave him a detailed brief about each and every staff of the branch. Though, he got the feedback from Mr. Goyal, but still he decided to judge each staff on his own independently without being biased by the feedback received, which was very helpful in creating a better team, because, some of the staff with negative feedback proved very nice and efficient workers.

Mr. Goyal suggested him that the branch was over staffed and the bank need to lay off some staff to maintain profitability. He told Vikram that business figures were very low and profits were at risk. He had motivated one staff to leave during the last February. He also advised Vikram that foreign exchange (forex) availability was a very big problem in the country and all the customers needed forex. In case, you open more accounts, you invite more problems in terms of forex demand. Advances figures were very low and credit deposit ratio was less than 3%. There were restrictions from Central Bank of the country to finance Retail and Wholesale trade. There was no scope for industrial advances. Main potential of business was tourism and Hotel industry.

It was the area earning forex and therefore, all bankers welcomed hotel accounts. Hotels needed Point of Sale facility to receive payment through Credit Cards, as their customers (tourist) will come with Credit Cards and therefore, they will keep their account with a bank having a Point of Sale facility. Vikram's bank did not have the Point of Sale facility and therefore, all the hotel owners refused to open account with them. All importers and big Corporates needed forex for their imports and therefore, they will seek commitment to provide them forex before opening their account. Some Corporate customers with expatriate workers would like to have a commitment to provide forex for payment of salary for their workers every month. They could not commit any forex. All big depositors will keep their deposit with a bank which could provide them forex. Forex earner bank will stipulate a condition on customers to keep a specified amount of deposit to get a specified amount of forex. Due to the lack of forex, there was no incentive for depositors to keep deposit with them or borrow money from them. In this way, they found that all the normal paths of business were closed. But, where there is a will, there is a way. The action plan started with the Personal Meeting with the Chief Executives of various organizations.

Vikram asked his secretary Vanisha to make a list of all Corporates, Parastatal organizations, high net worth customers of the bank, as well as other banks along with the name of their Chief Executives and fix up his appointment. He started meeting at least 3-4 Chief Executives daily, to explore the possibility of getting their business. He found from the initial few meetings that people do not know much about his bank. Most of them felt that it was a very small bank, may not be in position to provide corporate banking services. He started explaining the size and strength of the bank and the products and services provided by them. This field work was a big exercise. Every day, by evening, he would draft a letter on the discussions along with some additional information and next day the letter on the discussions/ minutes will go to the Chief Executive with whom he had met. He started getting response and his competitors became alert. They also started chasing him and started contacting their parties, so that parties do not shift. This exercise continued for more than a month.

He was still not satisfied with the outcome of efforts. The results were not very encouraging in terms of actual business. Neither deposits nor advances were moving ahead. He called a staff meeting and motivated them to do something to improve the business. All the staff members were requested to give suggestions and particularly, what are the main hindrances in their way for the business development. They pointed out several operational problems, which were beyond their control. There were several policy issues and Risk Management issues requiring his intervention and deliberations. He realized that things may not move as expected, unless, he resolves those issues. Some of the issues were policy issues, which, needed the approval of the Corporate Office Mumbai. He decided to move ahead after SWOT analysis.

SWOT Analysis

He discussed the business strategy in their staff meeting. They brain stormed and collected entire relevant information for the SWOT analysis.

SWOT Analyses
Strengths
Very good and dedicated staff
Ideally located branch in the market area
Excellent branch premises
Fully computerized branch
Locker facility available
India Based population of around 7000 out of 85000
Entire wholesale and retail business was dominated by South Indians
Entire construction business was dominated by Gujarati Indians
Most of the Financial Controllers in various organizations were Indians

- More than 2500 Indian workers in construction business
- No NPA (Non Performing assets)

Weakness

Lack of publicity and marketing

No ATM and Point of Sale (P.O.S) facility

No forex earner account to get forex for LCs and imports

Customer base was very low

Profitability was very low

Credit deposit Ratio was below 3%

Deposits and Advances were very low

Level of motivation and morale of staff was very low

Lack of direction and incentive to work

Lack of voluntary involvement of staff

Policy restrictions to increase business

Lack of reward

Declining business trend

Lack of high net worth customers

Opportunities

Remittance facility for the salary of Indian workers

Loan/Overdraft for wholesale and retail

L/C and Bank Guarantee facility for construction contractors

L/C facility for Importers

Collection of utility bills for telephone, electricity and water bills for PUC, Airtel and Cable & Wireless

Loans to Tourism Industry / Hotels

Offshore Banking

ATM/POS facility for Tourist and Hotel industry

Financing of Mortgage loan against commercial buildings

Personal loan to employees

Increase in number of account particularly for salaried employees

Threats

Competition

Very high risk in hotel financing
Externalization problem discourage financing in forex
Risk of default in forex loan even by Government and Parastatal Organisations
People change their jobs frequently resulting in risk of default in Retail Personal loans
No avenue for deployment of surplus funds
Treasury Bills/Bonds were not available on demand
Central Bank restriction on financing Retail/Wholesale

After discussion of SWOT in the staff meeting, it was unanimously resolved by the team that they shall double their customer base within one year. Loan policy had one positive point that personal loan could be sanctioned upto rupees 50, 000/- on clean basis. Initially, they identified the area of retail loans to increase advances. They resolved to sanction, at least 30 loans in a month.

Chapter 2

IRON OUT THE HURDLES

Points to ponder

- Appropriate person at the appropriate place
- Be practical, while fixing policy norms
- Superior office need to respond fast
- Help your subordinates to perform
- Remove the hurdles in performance
- Be flexible
- Positive attitude to take Risk
- Manage the Risk
- Find the way out
- Never discourage staff by saying no, unless there is justified reason to refuse
- Seek suggestions from the staff
- Ask the staff for hurdles in operation

Vikram realized that it was his duty as the Chief Executive to remove the hurdles from business development and give a go ahead to his staff, wherever they bring a problem to him. The biggest hurdle was the loan policy of the territory. It was so stringent that one cannot perform, even if, he wants. It was framed, keeping in view a very high level of existing business figures. Where, there are business figures in several hundred million or billions, the caps imposed in percentage terms on exposure may make a sense. But, when the business figures are too low, the cap in percentage of total advances will be very negligible in total value terms. Total advances of the territory at that time were few million rupees. There was a cap of 5% in retail personal or clean loan, which will allow total loan in this category upto Rs.350, 000/- only against the total advances of seven million. After the sanction of seven loans of rupee 50,000/- each, the cap will be over and you cannot finance. If, anybody sees the total value of Rs.350, 000/- as exposure cap, it is negligible for a bank operating in a country. But, in terms of loan policy guidelines, it needed to be observed and adhered to strictly.

His predecessors were allowing clean personal loan upto Rs.5, 000/- only, repayable in 10 installments. It was very difficult for him to increase advances with this pace. Though, there was one product named loan for consumer durables with a limit of Rs.50, 000/- but, it needed a margin of 10% from the borrower. Borrower needed to bring quotation from the supplier and the disbursement of loan will be made directly to the supplier. It was a big hassle for the borrower. Nobody wants Hassels. Moreover, the consumer durable items in the market were in short supply, due to lack of forex. By the time, borrower get the banker's cheque, the item will be found already sold and the borrower will now keep on roaming around with the cheque to find the goods somewhere else. After finance, the bank need to inspect the goods to ensure the end use of funds and if the banker goes to his residence for inspection of goods financed under consumer durable scheme, the borrower feels offended,.

Keeping in view the problems, Vikram immediately reviewed the loan policy and incorporated all the changes required for him to develop business. All the exposure caps were recommended to be increased. Margin requirements and security norms were revised according to his professional and business prudence. The policy norms for the areas of scope for business development were accordingly modified in such a way that the policy could not restrict him, to increase business. He took only 2-3 days to overhaul the entire loan policy, to make it conducive for business development. But all the things could not move with his speed. Unless, there was an appropriate person at the appropriate place in the entire line assembly, momentum will stop. If you want a person to respond and clear the things, to help you perform at your speed, it may not always be possible. It happened here also. The loan policy could not be approved for more than a year. There were several queries. He tried to reply, all the queries the same day or the next day. But several authorities with different mind sets were involved and the process had to take its time.

He could not afford to wait for a period of one year for the approval of the policy. Each day and night was very valuable for him, his passion for business development and level of motivation developed in his staff team was so high that they went ahead with increase in advances and business as initially resolved by them in their staff meeting. Now, he was violating the caps of his old loan policy, but he was within the caps recommended by him in the proposed / revised policy. He was confident that the policy will be approved and all his actions will be ratified and confirmed by his General Manager (International Operations).

During a period of nine months ending March 07, they could disburse 374 loans and the total advances increased from Rs7 million to Rs.20 million. Their loan policy was still not approved and they exceeded the Personal loan exposure upto 30% of total advances as against the old cap of 5% and proposed cap of 40%. Their new General Manager (Intl. Ops) Mr. R.K. Bansal took over the charge and he asked Vikram about the pending issues. Mr. Bansal was really a practical and professional banker. He immediately expedited the issue and arranged to approve their loan policy with some changes. The exposure cap for clean loan was approved at 10% of total advances. He again recommend for the increase, providing the information that they have already crossed 30%. So their cap must not be less than 40%, otherwise, it will restrict them for business development. Immediately, it was approved encouraging him to go ahead for business development. The positive attitude and understanding the practical problems by Mr. R.K. Bansal motivated him to perform still better and now his staff team was also fully motivated to achieve new heights.

Vikram reviewed all the policies, one by one and removed all the restriction for business development but fully taking care of the risk management as a banker. Local staff policy was reviewed to provide more incentives to his dedicated and hardworking staff.

Removal of Operational Bottlenecks

It is very important to know about the bottlenecks. When one talk about the bottleneck, everybody knows that neck is always at the top of the bottle. Operational Staff wants to perform, but the Chief Executive may be the neck of the bottle. One has to be very practical in his approach towards the operational problems. One of the supervisors brought to the knowledge of Mr. Vikram that the people borrowing money do not have margin money. There was no saving culture in the country. Everybody wanted loan without margin. Any loan product stipulating margin had a problem of popularity. Vikram decided to focus on personal loans, instead of asset based loan upto SR50, 000/-. His supervisors brought to his knowledge that there were many housing loan borrowers, who have already bought a plot from their own sources, but now they do not have margin to contribute for the building. They discussed if it was possible to accept the amount spent on buying the plot as margin money and finally, it was resolved to consider the same and finance such cases.

There were certain cases; the plot was in the name of mother who was not earning. Son or daughters wanted to build a house on the land. Mother was ready to create mortgage of property and become joint borrower. Singly, mother could not borrow in the absence of income and son/daughter could not be borrower because they did not own the land. They were allowed loan in the joint name of mother and son. Recovery could be made for the salary of son.

According to the usual norms, the borrower and the guarantor had to be a Government or Parastatal employee. Sometimes, the supervisors would come to him that they were not in a position to find a guarantor working with Government or Parastatal organization. Vikram would ask him to find a reputed businessman to guarantee the loan or an employee of a reputed private organization. Sometimes, the supervisor will ask him that the borrower was working with a private employer, who was reputed one. He would ask him to find a guarantor working with the Government or Parastatal and assign their salary. In this way, they would try to help maximum of their borrowers to give them alternatives and manage their risk as well.

Initially, bank was stipulating one guarantor for a loan. It was observed that some people leave the job frequently and even guarantor had left the job creating a problem in recovery. It was decided to ask for two guarantors, working with the Government or Parastatal. Now, the bank was more secure. In case the borrower leaves the job and defaults in repayment, they would invoke the guarantee of the guarantor and write to his employer to remit the loan installment after deduction from his salary. As soon as the salary of guarantor was deducted, he would put pressure on the borrower for repayment and default will be avoided soon.

Supervisors brought to his knowledge that some of the borrowers/guarantors changed their job and did not assign the salary of the new job. They started taking one additional salary assignment, keeping the name of the employer blank. As soon as the operational team brought their problems, they would discuss and find a solution for risk management and constant business development.

Vikram would never hesitate to take risk and always try to remove the bottleneck in the operations. In this way, he motivated his staff to work with positive attitude and trained them in risk management as well. But, any defaulter of loan in the past or present would not be allowed to take loan in future.

Operational Staff was in direct contact of the customers and therefore, they will be getting real feedback from the customers. Customer feedback helped them to satisfy the customers. One day, one of the supervisors Mrs. Rosy came to him with a feed back. She told him that a customer was saying that they were happy that Bobby was advertising on TV. It was very good, but the minimum charges on sale of forex which were Rs.200/- were too high. Even if, a customer buy USD100/- from the bank, he was to pay Rs.200/- as minimum charges. Initially, the minimum charges were Rs.20/- only. These were increased due to the lack of forex to discourage people and also to increase profitability in the old regulated regime. Now the scenario had changed. Forex was available easily and there was no need to impose high charges. Bank had the liberty to decide the purchase and sale price of forex. Vikram himself was observing the trend of sale of forex. Demand had gone down. He was thinking to reduce the charges and make it cheaper to increase demand. He asked Rosy, what should be the reasonable charges? She said make it Rs.100/- or less. He immediately allowed to reduce the minimum charges from Rs 200 to Rs 20/-. It was a big relief to small customers buying forex upto USD1000/-.

Chapter 3

MARKETING AND PUBLICITY

Points to ponder

- Try to be in news for good products and services
- Use different mode of advertisement to reach every body
- Create your brand position in the minds of people
- Use cost effective advertisement tool with high impact
- Match customer responses with your market image built by advertisement
- Brief your staff about the product before advertisement
- Take care of Corporate Social Responsibility
- Keep thinking new ideas
- Change before the change
- Train your staff
- Delegate the job and powers
- Share the work among staff
- Devise check list
- Prepare pamphlets which are easy to understand
- Let all the staff be marketers
- Be fast in service delivery

- **Sometimes confirmation is easier than the prior approval**

Vikram very well knew that it was his responsibility to take care of the policy norms. He took a risk and gave a go ahead to his staff, before the approval of policy. Their self imposed targets to double the customer base within one year and sanction of minimum thirty loans in a month were very challenging. He had one (IBO) India based officer Mr. Siva. He was very hardworking, competent, sincere and devoted worker. He had three supervisors. Jullie Harison, the senior most Supervisor was looking after opening of new accounts, statistical returns for Central Bank of the country, joint custodian of cash, remittance and forex payments. A bit slow, but, very sincere, obedient and hardworking lady. Second Supervisor, Mrs. Rosy was looking after clearing operations, investments, standing orders and credit department. A very hardworking, sincere, devoted and obedient worker. She kept a perfect watch on investment portfolio, balances with Central Bank and vigorous follow up of advances. She will not allow a customer to default and delay in repayment of installment. Third Supervisor, Ms Leena Harrow, was very efficient and sincere worker. She was looking after entire payments and receipts, forex department, Bills, LCs, Internet banking and Computer Data Base Administrator. She will also check in the posting log of the entire day in the evening.

All the three supervisor were preoccupied with various routine of their respective departments. It was very difficult to spare a supervisor to process 30 loan applications in a month. They decided that all the three supervisors will process loan application, whosoever is approached by the borrower for a loan; she will process the application of retail loan. Though, the credit department basically remained with Rosy. Now, the main issue was to get ample loan applications. They prepared a one page chart of their loan products specifying limit, rate of interest, security, margin and main conditions. Now, they again started contacting Chief Executives of various organizations with a request to arrange a meeting with their staff to make a presentation on loans and other bank products. It was to be a staff welfare measure on their part. Vikram started making presentation along with one of the Supervisors, turn by turn and his driver Rishi.

After a few presentations, all the supervisors and even his driver became expert in making presentations. Some clerks were also trained in making presentations. These presentations started yielding results and they started opening many new accounts for granting loans. Each loan application took two days for sanction and disbursement. It was so fast that existing borrowers started making word of mouth publicity among their colleagues. People started talking in the market that Bobby Bank is giving easy loans at a very fast speed. No other bank in the country was so fast, in processing of loan applications. It increased the market image of the bank and business figures showed the change.

Marketing tools

Marketing tools are very important. It is not necessary to spend big amounts on advertisement and publicity.

Sometimes small things make an impact. One day an idea came into the mind of Vikram that they should put a banner on the glass inside the branch, so that people on the road can read it. They prepared two banners of the size one meter x half meter. It costed Rs.324/- each banner. It was as under –

Bobby International Bank

Welcomes

You

to open your account

and

Avail easy loan schemes of Bobby

These two banners made charismatic impact on the public. Immediately, they started getting many people for opening their accounts and requests for loans. Now, they stopped making presentations. They started getting ample applications. Loan disbursements during some of the months, were more than 60 applications.

Similarly, one day, again an idea came into his mind that forex inflow of their bank was too low; tourist did not come to them to sell forex. Why should they not put a banner for attracting tourist? He again called the Printer and asked him to prepare two banners of the same size with the following message –

STEP IN FOR MONEY CHANGE

BOBBY INTERNATIONAL BANK

Immediately, after putting this banner, more tourists started coming to bank and the flow of forex increased substantially.

One day, an idea came to his mind that there were two telecom service providers, but none of them was exploring advertising through SMS message. Vikram had good relations with the Chief Executive and the Financial Controller of Airtel. He gave them an idea to advertise through bulk SMS message. They liked the idea and he gave three messages to popularize their Loan and Deposit products. They made these three messages complimentary, without any charge. As soon as, their first message flashed, all their telephones started ringing for enquiries. Their entire staff was aware of the products and therefore, who-so-ever lifted the phone, replied to the customers. All the publicity was equally and efficiently responded in action by the staff. It resulted in improving the image of the bank in the market. News paper media was costing Rs.350/- for $1/8^{th}$ page and Rs.600/- for a $1/4^{th}$ page in The Nation daily. They started using it to popularize their products and services. Keeping in view the developing trend, publicity budget was proposed for increase and Vikram decided to go for TV advertisement. A special advertisement clip of 38 second was made, showing the working of the staff with the following message

---

Bobby International Bank

100 years banking with Passion

Bobby Sun, a symbol of progress and prosperity for its 43 million customers. A Bank with efficiency and speed of the present and great values of past 100 years, high-tech – high touch, friendly, informal, accessible, affordable, State of the Art and Straight from the Heart.

Visit Bobby for its best of class banking experience.

Feel the change.

Now the people started talking in the market saying, Bobby has transformed. There was really a visible change in the business, style of business, speed of responses, service quality and market perception.

Referral Marketing

Vikram dealt with all high profile customers personally and they brought more customers from their circle. Who so ever came to the bank once, he will bring more customers from his circle of friends and relatives. Many times, he needed to help some customers for their banking needs elsewhere; it may not be a direct benefit. But after some time, he will open his account and give business for sure.

Press, Media and New Initiatives

It is very important to go for press conference. It gives a good publicity free of cost. Vikram would always find a reason for press conference. He went for press conference, when he launched Core Banking Solution in August 2007. They launched internet banking in April 2008 and again called a press conference. In 2008, they celebrated their centenary and again press conference was arranged. Their Executive Director visited the territory and they arranged press conference. All these press meets improved the market image of the bank and they remained in news frequently.

New initiatives are a must to attract the attention of the public. Every time a new initiative was launched, it gave an opportunity to approach press and media. It popularized their brand, as well as other products and services. They launched Core Banking Solution, Internet Banking, Loan against property, Loan against future rent accruals, Rapid Transfer of Fund to India.

Customer Meets

Once in a month or two, customer meet was arranged to get feedback and understanding their problems. They got many valuable suggestions from the customers. Customers pointed out their weaknesses in the meet and it gave an opportunity to improve. They got perception of customers about their products, services and service charges. Many times common customers of other banks provided information about bank's competitors, which was very difficult to get otherwise. The information on competitors was very important to devise his strategy to fight competition.

Creole Festival celebrations

They decided in their staff meeting to participate in the Creole festival in 2008. Staff also enjoyed the festival and participated with full enthusiasm. Many people visited Bank's stall and they got good publicity.

Ideas & Constant Change

"There is nothing as powerful as an idea whose time has come"- Victor Hugo. One more great personality Swami Vivekanand has said that take up one idea, make that idea your life, think of it, dream of it, live on that idea. Let the brain, muscles, nerves, every part of your body be full of that idea alone. This is the way great spiritual giants are produced.

Ideas can change the life. A business organization needs constant change to stay going. Old cells are bound to die and new cells need to take their place. Nobody has the monopoly on ideas. Any staff member can give good idea, which can work to boost your business. Bank's staff meetings were very good to generate ideas. Once, they were discussing in a staff meeting that people did not know much about Bobby bank. One of the staff suggested that they should celebrate Creole Festival and put up a stall in the festival. Other staff suggested selling some publicity material of the bank for charity. It was a good idea. Vikram liked the idea. But Financial Institution Act of the country did not allow the banks to be involved in sale/purchase of goods. It was subject to penalty and punishment from Central Bank of the country. Vikram wrote a formal letter to the Central Bank of the country to allow Bobby to put up a stall in the festival and sell publicity material for charity purposes. They got the permission.

The festival was arranged by the Govt. of the country. They immediately made a small Committee of three staff members to make it happen successfully. It was for the first time, Bobby bank decided to participate in the festival. They discussed and decided five items to be imported from India; T-shirts with Bank's logo in front and Creole festival logo on the back. Umbrella with bank's logo, Metal key ring cum bottle opener, pen, Caps and balloons for the kids. It was Vikram's duty to arrange these items from India. He contacted some dealers and got their quotations. After discussion with the suppliers, balloon and caps were dropped and other four items were ordered. Supplier sent photographs of the items but quality of the items could not be verified by photograph. It was a matter of reputation of the bank as well as India, as the goods were imported from India. Vikram had to ensure that the best quality goods are imported and the price must be reasonable according to the quality.

He requested one of the Branch Managers in New Delhi near the office of the supplier to check the quality of goods and the price quoted by the party. Supplier was asked to show the samples to the Branch Manager. He rejected the initial samples of T-shirt and Umbrella. Supplier again brought some more sample and then ultimately the final choice was made. The process of preparation of sample and their selection took one and half month. By the time, goods were ready; around 50 days were left for the festival. There was no direct shipment from Mumbai to this place. It was to come through South Africa or Dubai. Minimum time required was 45 days. It was a big risk. If goods do not reach in time, there was no use. Entire preparation would go waste. They reduced the quantity and asked the supplier to dispatch goods by Air Cargo. Vikram kept on following up with supplier and they received the goods in time. Staff team identified for the job was following up with the Govt. to allot a stall. Bank sponsored some prizes for the kids performing in the festival, which enabled them to get the stall free of any rent. Festival was for a week. Staff team decided their turn to be present on the stall. Three staff would remain present from 8 AM to 10 PM. Other staff would also be visiting the stall for some time during the day, daily. It was a successful participation. Bank sent SMS messages for inviting public to visit bank's stall. It was a big publicity initiative. Govt. of the country appreciated their efforts to participate in the festival. Sales proceeds were donated to take care of their Corporate Social Responsibility.

Vikram was exploring the option of publicity at the lowest cost. Idea of putting a banner to welcome people for opening an account and avail easy loan schemes of Bobby came to his mind. When they put two banners costing Rs.650/- only, the impact was visible and unexpected. People had an impression that Bank does not want to open fresh accounts. They started getting 15-20 accounts daily after putting these banners. Many of these customers were potential borrowers for personal loan. Similarly, after putting banner for Money Change, flow of tourists increased in the branch and forex inflow improved a lot.

In one of the staff meeting, they were discussing about the delay in issue of identity cards to their customers. Lamination of the card was a simple job, but, it was taking time, because, the party, doing the job was very slow. One of their staff members suggested buying a lamination machine. Vikram immediately decided to import the machine and hence, they imported a machine and started in house lamination. It facilitated the work faster and lowered the cost as well. Vikram was thinking of an idea of a low cost advertisement. They needed an advertisement at least cost with maximum effect. The idea of SMS messages was a good publicity at low cost.

Similarly, when they decided to go for TV advertisement, Vikram found that TV advertisement was very cheap in the country. They decided to project their bank and the staff working in normal course. All the staff members were projected in the advertisement. Many people started knowing the bank's staff due to TV commercial.

Chapter 4

Staff Precious Asset

Points to ponder

- **Love your staff**
- **Fun and Frolic**
- **Team Building**
- **Mix up with staff**
- **Give benefits with open heart**
- **Make them feel you care for them**
- **Educate your staff**
- **Training and development**
- **Mentoring**
- **Involve in decision making**
- **Appreciate the good work and hard work**
- **Delegate and empower**

It is the staff of an organization, which ensures right side of your balance sheet is fully left and left side of your balance sheet is fully right. It does not figure in the right side of your balance sheet itself, but still has much more weight than the tangible assets. Fully motivated and passionate staff makes things happen. They turn impossible into possible. A good leader needs to have a very high level of Emotional Quotient.

Managing Emotions in the human relationships has crucial role. Many times, when, it comes to staff relations, Vikram worked with his heart instead of mind. It paid rich reward. Wherever, a staff commited a mistake and Vikram found the mistake, his first priority was to educate his staff to learn from the mistake and avoid repetition. It was not necessary to humiliate or fire the staff for mistake. If, he signed a paper with mistake and it is identified later on, he will own the mistake, instead of blaming his staff, but definitely advise his staff to learn from it. In almost all the interactions with the staff, he would first analyze the impact of his response on the feelings of his staff.

Love begets love. Vikram loved his staff and his staff loved him. Anybody will have a tendency to sacrifice in love. It is a universal fact. If the staff is happy, the performance will be better. They will work more, sincerity and devotion will increase and ultimately, performance will have positive impact. When the staff is self motivated and passionate about the work, they enjoy their work and do not get tired. It increases the output and job satisfaction.

Once, one of the Supervisors, Mrs. Rosy, who was looking after advances department, had to prepare a return. The statistical return named DSB, which was statutory, to be submitted to Reserve Bank of India. Rosy was so busy during the entire operations that it was not possible for her to find time. All the three Supervisors were working late, till 7 PM as a matter of routine. There was a reminder from Central Office Mumbai for the DSB Return and Vikram advised Rosy that they need to send the return early as there was a reminder. It was Saturday and normal working hours on Saturdays were from 9 am to 11am. After the routine was over, Rosy started completing DSB Return. It was a tough and time consuming job. She kept on working on the return, till 8 pm in the evening. Vikram was so impressed by the hard work and dedication that when she finished the job at 8 pm, they were three people in the branch. He appreciated her for the hard work saying that Rosy, you have won his heart. You are so dedicated and hard working. Vikram expressed his love for Rosy due to her hard work. She felt very happy and Vikram's heart was filled with parental love and Rosy was further motivated to work harder. Apart from Clearing Operations, fund management and investments, she handled more than 800 loan accounts and every month, she would prepare review proposals of 50-60 accounts apart from processing fresh loan applications.

Team Building

In view of team building strategy, Vikram proposed a staff picnic. His staff was well trained in managing such events. They planned everything. Each staff was allocated some items to prepare and bring in the picnic. Vikram was allotted Indian Chapattis and (Chana Masala) white Gram Curry made with spices. He further provided them a bottle of Whisky. They bought Soft drink, beer, juice, fish and ice. A Pick-up was arranged to carry entire material to Port Lunay Beach. All the staff members enjoyed at the beach full day. It was a memorable event and it helped them in strengthening their cohesive teams.

Vikram observed that his staff was the hardest working and devoted among all the banks in the country. It was his pleasure to do something good to benefit his staff, while reviewing the local staff policy. Whatever ideas came to his mind and suggestions received from the staff, he tried to incorporate changes to benefit his staff with open heart. Bank could increase and double its profit within a performance period of nine month, in the first financial year and within a period of three years, their profits grew by ten times. It was the result of the strategy and vision supported by the hard work, dedication and passion of bank staff. They deserved the fruit. Rate of interest on staff loans were reduced from 10% to 8% and then again 8% to 6%. Loan limits were increased, salary was revised and increased by 25% with some new allowances, and Bonus was doubled twice. Leave travel concession facility was introduced. Leave encashment increased from 7 days a year to 21 days a year. They started feeling that they are being taken care of by the Management. When, they proposed the salary hike, they never expected that it could be approved so fast. Previous salary hike took three years to approve. This time, it was done within a month. Staff was surprised and started believing that Vikram had good image in Mumbai Office and he can get the things done from higher authorities very fast. Since, the performance of the territory was very good, Central Office of the bank was very positive and supportive of all his moves and whatever he proposed, his General Manager International Operation approved as early as possible. It boosted the motivation and morale of his team. Entire staff was now working with a killing instinct. It developed love and respect for management in the heart and mind of staff team.

Fun & Frolic

Visit to Praslin for picnic

May Day was an opportunity for the staff to enjoy and celebrate. Staff wanted to go for a picnic to another islands Praslin and La Dique and stay for a night. Praslin is a small island with a population of approx 7500 and La Dique was even a smaller island with a population of Approx 3500. It is considered a remote rural island. Beaches of La Dique are one among the best in the world. Lot of tourists visit the places and beaches of these two islands due to their beauty and clarity of water. There are a lot of hotels to stay. Most of the tourists visiting the country will certainly visit both these islands. Staff was ready to contribute some money to meet the cost of the trip, but, it was not enough to take care of the entire budget. Hotel stay and the transportation cost were too high to afford with the money contributed by the staff. One of their customer and friend Ms Loveleen had a hotel at Praslin i.e. the other island where the staff wanted to go for the picnic. Vikram discussed with her, if, she can make some concession for the stay and food for their staff. She was a very good friend of staff and therefore, she was excited on the news of the proposed staff party. She voluntarily offered that she will make the stay complementary. They needed to bear the cost of food only. Balance of the budget was sanctioned by Vikram as the Chief executive, so that staff enjoys the visit properly. It was a very big rebate and the staff was happy. They started planning each and every activity in advance. Tickets were booked by a Ferry. All other articles required for the event were arranged. Vikram offered whisky and wine for the staff to enjoy during the stay. All the staff members with their families were advised to be present at the jetty in the morning at the scheduled time of the ferry. Everybody came in time and as soon as the ferry came, all the staff boarded it. It was a beautiful boat, well maintained and very comfortable to sit. Seat numbers were allotted to all the passengers. All the passengers got their seats. Some of the seats remained vacant and the staff had an opportunity to take another seat of their choice and change according to their convenience. As soon as the ferry started the journey, their counter selling snacks started working and people started buying the snacks, cold drinks, bear etc. of their choice. Sea was calm at that time. As soon as the boat went deeper, the sea started showing higher waves. Fishes were flying in the air and coming down again in the water. Birds were catching fish in the water. Flocks of birds were seen in the sea. All the passengers were in the mood to enjoy and started singing songs. It was a journey of approx forty five minutes. Everybody enjoyed it. Ferry reached Praslin after forty five minutes and everybody came down on the jetty. Hotel had already sent the cars to receive at the jetty. Entire luggage was loaded in the cars and after fifteen minutes drive, they reached the hotel. It was a festive atmosphere. All the staff members were offered lemon tea as soon as they landed at the hotel. Everybody was allotted a room. After relaxing a bit in the room they proceeded to a beach. Everybody took bath in the sea and enjoyed at the beach. Evening was even more charming. A music party was invited and very good singers along with their instrument were present and started singing. Dinner was also ready side by side. Staff also started singing along with the singers while drinking. It was a very warm sweet evening and everybody forgot their entire worries. Everybody was in good mood. Eating and drinking kept on till late night unless everybody was tired of singing and dancing. It was a memorable evening and entire staff still misses the enjoyable moments. Next day, there was a plan to go to La Dique. Everybody was ready at the specified time and hotel cars dropped them at the jetty from where, a boat for La Dique was to go. It was a journey of fifteen minutes. The boat was very small in comparison to the ferry for Praslin. One of the family members of a staff had a shop of take away at La Dique. It was her duty to supply food for all the members from the take away shop. Order was placed well in advance to prepare the food for the entire team. After reaching La Dique, they straight away went to the beach. They set under the shade of a big tree on the beach. It was one of the best beaches of the world. Water was very clear. Fish were seen swimming in the water. Some of the staff members started taking bath in the sea. Lunch was served on the beach and it was an informal atmosphere. Staff started cracking jokes and singing songs. In the afternoon, they started their journey back to their place. When they started back from Praslin, it was evening. The sea became rough. Sea waves were hitting their ferry with big force. Ferry was shaking due to high and big waves of the sea. Some of the people went on the top of the ferry to enjoy the waves and the cool breeze. Some people started feeling sea sickness and nausea. Some people were still enjoying the evening and the rough journey of the ferry. Ultimately, they reached home in the late evening. It was a memorable trip and left a positive mark on the minds of the staff.

Christmas Celebration

Christmas was a big festival of the country. It was celebrated every year with big pump and show. Staff requested Vikram to allow them to buy a Christmas tree, which he immediately allowed. Staff decorated their branch and the Christmas tree with lights. Special event was the staff Christmas party. A special budget was sanctioned by Mumbai Office for this party every year. All the staff members will eat, drink and dance in the party and it will go on, till midnight. In 2008, Vikram decided to do something new to test the cohesiveness of the team and have some more fun.

He asked his secretary to take fifteen white paper sheets and write the name of one staff on one sheet. All the staff members were advised to write feedback about all the colleagues except their own. Vikram's sheet was also there, to know the perception of his staff about him. Vikram got all the sheets and asked his secretary to type the feedback for each staff on a separate sheet and give it to him. Vikram was a good poet also. So, he wrote few lines about each staff member in a poetic style and gave title to each staff. All the titles were chosen suiting to their positive qualities and speaking good about the staff. Vikram told his staff that he has given nick-names to all of them and written few lines of poem on each one. While all the staff members were eating, drinking and dancing, Vikram was asked to reveal the nick-names given to each staff. One by one, he read his poetic lines about a staff member and asked who this was? As soon as he spoke the poetic feedback and nick-name, they will shout the name of the person. The feedback sheet along with nick-name was given to each staff. It was a big fun and the feedback was very good about each other. Vikram could never believe that his staff perceived him a very intelligent and strong manager which came in the feedback sheet. Vikram felt so happy about the cohesiveness of his team.

There was a practice to gift bottle of wine or whisky on Christmas festival. Bank also sends gifts to its good customers and some customers also send bottle of wine or whisky as a gift. Vikram was a non drinker and so was his assistant Mr. Siva. Whatever bottle of wine or whisky he received as gift, some of the bottles, he used to send gift to some of their customers and whatever is left, he would be providing a bottle to his staff once in a month or two for a picnic. Whenever, they were in celebration mood, they will get the bottle and there will be a staff party to enjoy the moments together in the late evening. Mr. Siva and Vikram will be taking a glass of juice or soft drink, while the other staff will enjoy whisky or wine with snacks. These informal moments were very precious for team building among all the staff. Vikram used these informal gatherings to share his strategy with his staff informally and briefing them about their competitors and their actions.

Educating and Mentoring of Staff

His assistant Mr. Siva was a very competent person and he would be doing a lot of work requiring high level of skill and mind. Vikram advised him to delegate the job among staff and guide them to do. Let them learn more and more. He decided to include all the three Supervisor in Asset Liability Committee (ALCO) and brief them during ALCO meetings as to what was happening in the Economy, what were the pricing strategies. How do they decide the price of a product? How do they calculate the Prime Lending Rate? What are the important issues and what are their implications. Every month ALCO will meet and Vikram shall come out with the revised pricing of a product or service. He will explain them about the price elasticity of demand and importance of review of pricing. They will discuss and many times, they will not allow Vikram to increase the tariff of a particular product. There will be big discussions several times.

Vikram was very vigilant and kept on observing the vouchers and the mistake being committed by staff in different heads of accounts. During the monthly staff meeting, he will ask some banking questions and then explain them about the concept. Sometimes, he would seek new ideas and suggestions for business development or improvement of process and service delivery. His Endeavour will be to increase the skill and knowledge of his staff and keep on mentoring them constantly to enrich their skill, knowledge and experience.

Every staff meeting will have some input from his side to improve the knowledge of his staff, sometimes on banking, sometimes on management, sometime on Economics, sometimes on Psychology, sometimes on marketing, sometimes on strategy. Vikram also enjoyed sharing his knowledge with his staff. Rosy was looking after credit department apart from other departments. She was a senior secondary pass. She had never studied accountancy and Management accounting. Earlier, there were no big loan proposals and therefore, she had never processed big loans and was not aware of the interpretation of financial statements. Now, the business had started increasing and therefore some big loan proposals were also mobilized. Mr. Siva was very busy in several jobs and it was only Vikram, who could process the proposals. He could very well do it but he thought that his junior staff must be groomed to take higher responsibilities and learn more about the loan appraisals. He motivated Rosy to learn it. Rosy was very happy to learn but she needed to be explained about it. Vikram asked her to bring the balance sheet and profit and loss account of a party to process. He will explain her about various ratios to be calculated and the method of calculation. She started doing it. Initially, she told that she will calculate the ratios, but, she does not know the analysis and explanation about the particular ratio. After calculation of the ratios by Rosy, he will call her and explain the importance, impact and implication of a particular ratio. He will then dictate the language as what should be the explanation to justify the sanction of the loans. After three four proposals, in this way Rosy started processing and appraising the loan proposals herself. Sometimes, he will allot additional responsibilities to a staff and some time job rotation of the staff to learn about the working of the new departments. This is how; he groomed all the staff members wherever needed.

Help and Guidance in personal life of staff

Majority of the population of this country was Roman Catholic. Only five percent of the people will get married and sixty percent of the marriages failed. They will have living relationship of boyfriend and girlfriend. One of the lady staff members had a boy friend. Who was a very nice man. Somehow, there was some problem in their relationship. The guy was a very gentle man. This girl was attracted to another man who was living in Italy. He had a wife in Italy and other girlfriends in this country. He was a customer of the bank. He will come to the bank for his banking dealings and flirt to please her. She stopped talking to her earlier boy friend, left his house and came to her mother's house. She was planning to be the girlfriend of the new guy. Vikram came to know of this incident. He asked his assistant Mr. Siva to tell him, as and when, this new guy visits the branch. After a day or two, the man came. Vikram observed him and found that there was no genuineness in his eyes. He will definitely deceive the girl. Vikram called that staff and shared his feelings that her earlier boy friend seems to be a genuine man and the new guy does not seem to be a genuine guy from his eyes, he will definitely deceive her, and she will repent later on. This new guy called her in a disco in the night, while he had called one more girl in the disco. She reached there and found the other girl as well along with him. She came back and next day she told Vikram that he was right. Vikram called her old boyfriend and asked them to unite and be friend again and after sometimes, they got married and they had a daughter in due course.

Chapter 5

SEARCH FOR THE NICHE

Points to ponder

- **Find, what your competitors cannot do**
- **Bring new products to have an edge**
- **Take new initiatives**
- **Synergies with other branches**
- **Look for avenues within existing circumstances**
- **Keep a constant watch on opportunities**
- **Liaisoning and networking**
- **Be pioneer**
- **Be proactive and resilient**
- **Fight for your share of cake**
- **Be focused and alert**

Initially, his predecessor explained him all the hindrances and problems in business development. The country had a very small population of 84000 people. There were no big industries in the country. Due to the ban on financing Retail and wholesale, business, advances could not increase and due to non availability of ATM / Point of Sale facility forex revenue was lacking. Apart from import, even individual customers were entitled to USD

400/- against production of travel ticket, as per government guidelines, but bank did not have ample forex to take care of the demand of USD400/- per travel ticket. As per the statistics of Statistical Bureau, around 40000 people traveled in a year. It was difficult to provide forex to all customers. All people having deposits needed forex for their business and they did not prefer Bobby, for want of forex. Barclays was granting personal loans upto rupees 100,000/- without personal guarantee. Vikram was not allowed to grant forex loans. Treasury Bills were not available freely to deploy surplus funds and therefore, surplus funds were lying idle in Central Bank. There was no incentive to increase deposits by paying higher rate of interest. Credit deposit ratio of the bank was 2.9% only. New accounts were not being opened, because of lack of forex.

In view of above scenario, it looked practically impossible to do something good for business development. It was a big question as to where to start and what to do. Almost all the areas looked blocked. Vikram started exploring the niche. In view of poor credit deposit ratio, he strongly believed that they should do something to increase advances. He observed that majority of the population in the country was employed and they did not have saving culture. They were the potential customers for loans. Personal loans were the most convenient loans, not requiring inspections and assets verifications. They decided to go for personal loans against the assignment of salary with one guarantor. Personal loan limit upto Rs. 50, 000/- was allowed under the loan policy. Main challenge was the competition from Barclays, which allowed personal loans upto rupees100, 000/- without third party guarantee. Vikram found that their response time for sanction of a loan was more than seven days. He relied on his speed and started disposing loan application within two days. Sometimes, they were in a position to disburse loan on the same day. As soon as the salary assignment of borrower and guarantor was confirmed by the Supervisor and mortgage insurance policy was issued by the insurance company, they disbursed the loan. The speed of sanction of loan was surprising and within few days, there was positive word of mouth publicity. SMS messages and display of banner outside the branch coupled with fast disposal of loan resulted in flow of good number of loan applications. People started talking in the market, if you want fast, go to Bobby.

Vikram observed that there were many people of Indian Origin. They were in business and needed loans for the business. They were not allowed to finance whole sale and retail business, but there was no restriction on granting loan against deposits to individuals. All these businessmen had their deposits in India with some banks. Vikram advised them to transfer their deposit in India from other bank to Bobby bank and avail loan against that deposit in rupee. Customer was allowed to keep the Indian rupee deposit in India and repay their rupee loan in rupee. In case of default, Indian deposit may be used to repay the loan. This was a unique facility, which only Bobby could provide and no other bank was in a position to provide it, therefore there was no competition in this area.

Then Vikram found that many people kept their forex deposits outside the country. They had branches in several countries, Vikram advised them to transfer their deposit with Bobby Bank branch outside the country and he would grant loans against the security of that deposit. In this way, he could mobilize deposits for his other territories and increased his credit portfolio on secured basis. Other banks could not provide this facility and he had an edge.

Their Core Banking Solution enabled them to launch a product Fund Transfer to India. It was an instant credit to the beneficiary account in India. He brought this product for transfer of funds to India. There were many Indian workers and employees with construction companies and some other employers, who were facing difficulty in transfer of salary. It was taking long time by demand drafts and very costly by SWIFT transfers. Vikram priced this product @ USD5/- per transfer which was much less than the cost of bank draft and SWIFT transfer and they could credit the beneficiary account in India immediately and give an acknowledgement to sender. He asked the employers to open a forex account with them, which increased their deposits and cost free funds in current account and the beneficiary was asked to open his account in Bobby Bank branches in India. In this way, he helped Indian branches to get business and got good commission on remittances. It was also their unique product; no other bank could provide this facility.

One of the initiatives, Vikram took about internet banking, though, it was view based only. Customer was in a position to see his statement of account or save/print his statement of account. No other bank in the country was allowing internet banking to individual customers. It was free of cost. It attracted customers using internet and they were pioneer in this product.

Due to the lack of forex, new savings accounts were discouraged in the past, but for granting new loans, they needed more and more customer to open account with them. Vikram knew that they could not provide USD 400/- on a ticket. There was no restriction on providing additional forex more than USD400/-. He started advising his customers to bring forex USD400/- from other bank and still he will give them USD100/- or USD200/-. It was an incentive, other bank's were not allowing any forex on a stamped ticket having issued USD400/-. Their customer will be getting USD500/- after they grant USD100/-. In this way, he satisfied four customers with USD400/- and earned commission four times. In this way, customer was happy to get additional forex. He was happy to use forex judiciously and earn four times commission, satisfying number of customers four times.

Vikram observed that many people had property as security and regular source of income also. They were not allowed to borrow for their business company for Working Capital. There was no ban on mortgage finance in the name of individuals. He developed two products **(1)** Loan against Property, **(2)** Advance against future rent accruals and got them approved from corporate office.

There were no hassles. After mortgage of the property, loan was credited to the account of borrower. Loan against property was very good, even as a replacement of Housing Loans. Because, Housing Loan disbursement was in stages and the borrower needed to submit bills etc. It worked well but the other scheme advance against future rent accrual did not work well because, it was linked with the future rent during the lease period and usually, people execute lease deed for a period of one year only. Therefore, within one year, eligibility of loan was not ample to make the product attractive.

Watch for the opportunities

As the beauty is short lived, similarly, opportunities are momentary. Many a times, opportunities come hidden in a problem. It is so embedded in the complex problem that anybody avoiding problems and or shirking responsibilities or who is not proactive in accepting the challenge will definitely miss it. One has to keep a constant watch to identify and encash the same. As a hunter keeps a watch and aim on its object and click the trigger as soon as, it comes in the range. Opportunity once lost, may never come again. Once, Exim Bank of India sanctioned a Line of Credit to the Govt. of the country for import of essential commodities from India. Vikram came to know about it and started keeping a watch over it. He requested the authorities to approach Bobby for opening Letter of Credits under the Line of Credit given by Exim Bank of India. Other bankers were also chasing for the business, because minimum commission on L/C would be USD160, 000/-. It was a big attraction.

Vikram's Profit for the year ending March 2007 was just double than that of March 2006. Target for 2008 was challenging. It was compulsory for Vikram to hunt for each and every avenue to increase profit.

Vikram started liaisoning with Exim Bank of India, High Commissioner of India to the country, Govt. of the country and the State Trading Co. who was to really utilize the L/C. Somehow, Govt. of the country chose a subsidiary of Standard Chartered Bank for opening L/Cs under the Line of Credit and informed Exim Bank of India about its decision. Because, this subsidiary had a shareholding of the government. Exim Bank wrote back to the Govt. that Bobby is their correspondent, why they want to choose other bank. He managed to get a copy of the letter. He immediately wrote a letter to the Govt. of the country, protesting strongly that they cannot use other bank for the transaction. Bobby will open L/C under the Line of Credit, as Exim Bank was their correspondent. Vikram requested the High Commissioner of India for the intervention. Ultimately Govt. of the country changed their decision and he got a letter that they are choosing Bobby for opening L/C under the Line of Credit facility. Vikram ultimately put up a proposal and got it sanctioned. Later on, he used this facility to pressurize Government for recovery of loan with their London Branch and part of the amount was recovered, He could surpass his profit target.

Govt. of the country started liberalization of the Economy. They allowed individuals to open their forex accounts. These forex accounts became unattractive due to imposition of Cash Reserve Ratio by the Central Bank on these forex deposits. Vikram was the first to go to public, welcoming them to open forex account. When rate of interest scenario went up due to implementation of IMF package, these forex depositors were motivated to convert their deposits to rupee and earn higher rate of interest. It worked well. They sold their forex to Bobby bank to avail higher rate of interest. They got forex, which was in short supply at that time.

Another opportunity came with the liberalization was the free trading of forex. Central Bank stopped deciding the rate of exchange and Rupee was put to free float as per the demand and supply of the market. They did not have much forex earner accounts, but now, he could pay higher price than other bank and buy forex. Bank was free to decide its buying and selling rate. They bought ample amount of forex and advertised in the paper.

Bobby International Bank

Offers

Liberal sale of forex upto USD200 even to non customers without any restriction.

More amount can be given as per genuineness of requirement

Contact Ph. ....

Public was surprised by this advertisement. Bank got many telephone calls to confirm, whether it is true. One of the news papers requested for written confirmation about the correctness of the news. Again, in the New Year, Vikram gave another advertisement in the paper regarding Sale of Forex which was as under –

Bobby International Bank

New Year Bonanza for importers and corporates

Bobby Offers

Liberal Sale of forex, open your account

And

Rush to avail.

Bobby Corporate Services,

Victoria……

Contact Ph. ………………..

These advertisements created vibrations in the market. Vikram was pioneer in advertising sale of forex, which was a scarce item for Bobby in the past. Even President of the country referred these advertisements in his address to the nation without naming the bank. Bank made a very good profit through forex trading. Market image of the bank improved a lot and Bobby had become the bank of first choice now.

In view of the economic reform programme, IMF had given targets of reserve money to Central Bank of the country. Central Bank was short of funds to achieve its targets of Reserve Money as on 31.03.2009. Governor, Central Bank requested Vikram to help and buy some forex from Central bank to the tune of USD 2 million. All the banks were tight in local currency resource at that time. His position was comfortable in this regard. Governor offered that CBS will buy back the forex at the same rate, if he did not need it. Vikram thought that it was his moral duty also, to help the Central Bank. Achievement of targets will help Central Bank to convince IMF that it was doing as per the projected targets. Vikram had the need for this forex and he could use it immediately. Central bank could achieve its target.

Sometimes people lose the opportunity. It happened with Vikram as well. It was matter of lack of proactiveness and slackness of formal style, on the part of the person. Bank had an account of a Church. They were very happy with the services and informal style of business. They had two more units or associate organizations having accounts with Barclays. They were not happy with Barclays due to their poor service and bureaucracy. One office bearer of each of their associate organizations visited Vikram personally for opening their account. As, all the signatories were not present and the resolution of the Managing Committee was not passed, he could not open their account. He filled in the account opening form, got their signatures and asked them to pass the resolution and get the signatures of other office bearers to open the account.

They were giving him a cheque of Rs.2 million for deposit in the new account to collect it from Barclays.

He did not take the cheque stating that they can give the cheque later on, when, all the signatories sign the account opening form and resolution is passed. Later on, they went to Barclays to meet their Manager and never came back him. Next day, Vikram realised his mistake. He had lost the opportunity by that time. He should have been proactive in accepting the cheque and the account could have been made operative after getting resolution and all papers. In fact, it was not his actual style of working, which, he did that day. It was a big lesson for him.

CHAPTER 6

MANAGING PROFITS

Points to ponder

- **Constant review of price of products and services**
- **Management of funds**
- **Comparison with competitors price**
- **Study price elasticity of demand**
- **No under pricing or over pricing**
- **Take Risk prudently to increase profit**
- **Think alternatives before taking risk**

Business organizations run on profit motive. Bank is not a charity organization and therefore, profit is a must to run the organization. A horse cannot have friendship with the grass, otherwise, it will die. Similarly, the business has to earn profit from the customers. This principle does not work well always. Many times, bank gets some important, high profile customers. If bank make concessions or exemptions of charges in these cases, it is not a cost, but, an investment. Sometimes, Vikram will decide to provide a service to a customer, free of cost. It is not the money which matters but the respect, the bank give to the customer by making it free. Vikram was smart enough to win the heart of some big customers by these small gestures. It gave big word of mouth publicity, which was helpful in image building of the bank.

When, Vikram took over the charge of the territory, profit was very low and the bank could not achieve its profit target in 2006. His predecessor, Mr. Goyal had briefed him about the constraints in business and difficulties in achievement of profit targets. Vikram could understand the limitations. Still, he was determined to achieve profit targets. It was very difficult to achieve the target with old styles and systems. It needed a strategic move to go ahead. He had the advantage of having a very competent, hardworking and dedicated Assistant Manager – Mr. Siva. He would come out with an idea, by which profit will increase. They will discuss the same. Then, they will discuss the idea into their ALCO meeting with their Supervisors and implement it. Every month there will be an ALCO meeting and his focus will be to review the pricing of different products and services

Constant Review of Pricing

Initially, the interest on Personal Loan was 10% and the loan for consumer durables was 9.5%. They increased the rate of personal loan to 12% and then slowly consumer durable loan was also increased to 12%. When, Central Bank increased the minimum rate of interest on deposits from 2.5% to 3.5%, they increased the interest from 12% to 15% to absorb the additional cost of deposits. They were charging interest on loans @ 8% which was increased to 10%. All overdraft limits were charged between 8-10% which was increased to 11.5%.

Vikram observed that the retail loans have the maximum potential to earn higher rate of interest. While other banks were lending @ 6-7% on big loans, he was focusing on retail loans @ 15%. It was the beginning of their campaign to increase retail loans and every month they were disbursing good number of loans. He observed that their processing charges were very low. They were charging procession fee at rupees200/- per hundred thousand. Vikram proposed to increase it. They discussed in ALCO meeting and increased the processing charges. They made various slabs of charges with a minimum of Rs.100/- and maximum of Rs.300/-. He again observed that still, there was a room for increase and the customers do not mind paying little more. Ultimately, they increased the processing fee to Rs.1000/- for a loan of SR50, 000/-and above. He observed that processing fee of Rs1000/- for small loans upto SR50,000/- was good from profitability angle, but a fee of rupees200/- per hundred thousand was very low in comparison to a processing of 1% being charged by other banks. Initially, he was using the lower processing fee as a unique selling point for popularizing his loans, later on, he increased it to 1% in line with other banks to manage and increase his profitability.

In the beginning, they were not charging processing charges on loan against banks own deposit lying with other branches. When he observed that the cases of loan against deposit of other branches are increasing, he started charging normal processing charges.

They were charging a penalty of rupees two hundred for return of cheque for financial reason. Customers were not bothered about the return of cheque. Many cheques were returned unpaid. They increased the charges from rupees200/- per instrument to SR250/- per instrument. Some other banks were also charging SR250/- and therefore, he was not out of the market rates. Similarly, cheque book charges were fixed long back and they were charging rupees sixty for a cheque book of 100 leaves. They reviewed it and increased to SR100/- for 100 leaves.

Forex was a precious item and they were selling forex with a commission of 1% Min Rs20/-. This service was totally price inelastic at that time. People will not mind paying higher charges, if they get the forex. Bank was selling forex @ Rs8/- a dollar while black market rate of dollar was Rs13/-. Vikram proposed to increase the minimum charges on currency sale from Rs20/- to Rs100/-. They discussed in their ALCO Meeting but the supervisors did not agree, they agreed for Rs50/- only. After few months, he again proposed to increase it to SR100-. Vikram asked the supervisors, if there was any complaint by any customer due to increase in fee, they said there was no complained and therefore, this time they agreed to increase it to Rs100/-.

Vikram still found that there was a room to increase. After few months he again proposed to increase it to Rs150/-. It was discussed in ALCO and they decided to increase in two slabs. They decided to keep Rs100/- upto USD200/- and Rs150/- more than USD200/-. Finally, he proposed to increase it to SR200/- and they increased. In this way, the minimum charges on forex sale were increased to 10 times in several stages. It increased the commission income substantially and the charges were in line with other banks.

Every month, Vikram used to bring in ALCO meeting a product or service to review its price. There would be discussions. He would explain his staff about the price elasticity of demand of a product or pricing strategy behind the proposed pricing of a product or service. Sometimes, he would propose a very low price of a product as a penetration pricing strategy. Some other times, he would propose a high price of a product being monopolistic price.

They did not have much business of letter of credit and the commission of L/C was only 1%. Barclays was charging a commission of 3% and other banks were charging 2%. Vikram would always consider the charges of other competitors before deciding the price of a product. Their pricing will not be higher than others. It may be equal to their competitors. Their speed of service will be much faster than the competitors. Therefore, customer would prefer Bobby bank with same or lower charges but much faster speed; he reviewed and increased all the charges several times.

New Product Pricing

When they brought a new product named Fund Transfer to India, it was a unique product and other banks did not have similar product. Other banks were charging around US$30-40 for Swift transfer to India for Indian workers. Funds would reach after 3-4 days and USD10-20 would be deducted by the intermediary bank. Vikram observed that many times, the charges are borne by the poor employees. They priced their product for US$5 only. They would credit to their account in Bobby Bank, India immediately. It was very fast and cost effective for the beneficiaries. They could mobilize the accounts of their employers. Their Indian branches could get NRE deposits, and they could earn some profit in foreign exchange deals of buying and selling of

Indian Rupee against US Dollar. It resulted into a very good profit making business for the bank.

Treasury Profit

Government of the country had been making frequent payment to Apollo Hospital in India through Central Bank. They were using Swift facility. It was taking two to three days. Once they had to send some urgent payment, which was not possible through their Swift. They requested Vikram, if he could help them in effecting the payment immediately. He sent a TT in India and followed up with personal telephone call with their branch to effect the payment through RTGS. It was so fast and effective that they started routing all these payment through Bobby bank. They could earn treasury profit in buying and selling of Indian Rupee against US Dollar.

Fund Management

Management of NOSTRO balance was very important for profit planning. Funds were being kept idle overnight. Vikram started placing funds overnight. Rate of interest on USD/EUR/GBP were reasonable and they started earning USD 50 – 100 per day. As their business increased, balances in Nostro Accounts also increased. Now the overnight placement could fetch interest on overnight placements between USD400 – 500. It continued for a long time unless Fed Rate had gone down to almost zero.

Management of local funds also played an important role. Those days, they were getting interest on their balances in current account with Central Bank. Vikram started monitoring the cash balances on daily basis. Even current deposits with Central Bank for temporary period would fetch interest @ 5.25% on excess credit balances. They focused more and more on current deposits which were free of cost. These resulted in increase of interest earned on Central Bank balances.

Scenario changed with the liberalization of economy in Nov. 2008. Now, Central Bank stopped remunerating the current account balances. Cash Ratio was increased from 5% to 13%. Even forex deposits were subject to Cash Reserve Ratio to be kept in local currency. A new facility of Deposit Auction Arrangement (DAA) was started for placing funds with Central Bank for a period of 7 days, 14 days and 28 days through weekly bids. DAA balances were neither considered for Cash Reserve Ratio nor Local Asset Ratio (LAR) also known as Statutory Liquidity Ratio. Central Bank stopped lending to Commercial Banks which was its function as the lender of last Resort. Weekly auction of Treasury Bills also started by Central Bank. Every week, Vikram would discuss with the supervisors and Asstt. Manager about the rate of bid. If they bid very high, they ran a risk of rejection of the bid and if they bid very low, there was loss of profit. He would take into account the recommendation of IMF, total size of the issue, liquidity position of fellow bankers. Most of the times their bids were more than the average tender price and never had a chance to keep idle funds due to non acceptance of bid.

Treasury Bills bid were asked on Friday and settlement was on Wednesday, while DAA bids were called on Wednesday and settlement on the same day. They planned to put high interest rate in Treasury Bills. If not accepted, they had the other opportunity of DAA. In this way, they tried to get maximum interest by putting higher rate bid and managing their risk.

Now they had to manage their liquidity in the absence of lending from Central Bank. They were keeping Rs10 – 15 million cushion for liquidity. Three other banks were short of liquidity and therefore, they would ask for the borrowing. They would lend the surplus funds with a condition to call back on any day, if needed; it resulted in increase of income from Money Market deals.

Currency Trading

After liberalization of the forex market and lifting of certain restriction on forex trading, it was a potential area to make profit. Initially, the market was volatile and all the banks kept a big margin in buying and selling of currency. Currency trading margin were as high as 20% and TT trading margin were around 13 – 14%. High margins gave them an opportunity to quote high rate of buying a currency and reduce the rate while selling it. Vikram decided that the rates shown on their board will be the best rates. Keeping in view the demand and supply of foreign currency, they would increase their buying price by even one rupee on dollar, still they made reasonable profit. As the market started stabilizing, they started reducing the selling rate. Gradually, their buying rate was highest and selling rate lowest among all the banks to avail the benefit of volume. Vikram started playing on a very thin margin and increased his volume. Therefore, most of the customers whether buying or selling the currency will prefer this bank.

Chapter 7

INFORMALITY AND FLEXIBILITY

Points to ponder

- **Be accessible as fast as possible**
- **Be informal**
- **Be flexible in applying rules and procedures**
- **Propose multiple solutions to customers**
- **Help the customer in choosing the best option**
- **Create value for the customer**
- **Forgo short term gain for long term gain**
- **Be positive in solving problems**

Vikram observed during the initial period of his posting that most of the Chief Executives of banks were not accessible. Their customers needed prior appointment of 10-15 days. It was a big problem for the customers. Particularly, in banking industry, many times, the customer will have a problem, which needs immediate solution. If the customer is asked to wait for 10-15 days, the purpose is defeated. In almost all the banks, it was difficult for a customer to meet the Chief Executive. They would be meeting the front line staff or the immediate next Manager. Many times, the

Manager does not have the powers to take care of the request of the customer. It creates unrest in the mind of a customer. Multi layer organizations are usually suffering from this problem. Vikram decided to make himself available to his customers any day and time, as long as, he was in the branch. Customers could freely step into his cabin and discuss their problems. As far as possible, he will try to solve their problem. He would always try to give several options to the customer to choose the best suitable one. The customer may not be in a position to take a decision as to which solution is the most suitable for him. He would help him choosing the best one by explaining the pros and cones of various options.

All his staff members knew that he does not need prior appointment for his customers and therefore, within a short period, public came to know that Bobby Bank is very informal. People started talking in the market, you can meet Bobby's CEO any time, and any dissatisfied customer of another bank would come to him. He tried to keep his responses very fast to meet the expectations of his customers.

Once, a customer needed a bank guarantee of rupee one million to start his Destination Management Company (DMC). He had applied for this facility with Barclays Bank as well as one other bank. It was in the process and taking long time. The customer was not satisfied with the speed. He met Vikram and explained his problem. Vikram discussed his proposal and security aspect and then asked him, how fast he needed it. The customer replied, if he gets in two days, he will be happy. The customer had Euro Deposit account with the bank. Vikram asked him, if it was possible to keep the security of Euro Deposit, till the mortgage papers are ready and signed. He had no problem. Vikram asked his supervisor to process the proposal for issue of guarantee. He kept a margin of 100% on Euro Deposit and issued the guarantee on the same day. It was agreed that the bank would release the margin after the mortgage formalities are completed. Vikram asked the customer to collect the guarantee by evening, on the same day. He issued the guarantee on the same day. The customer did not turn up to collect the guarantee. Next day morning, the customer came and collected the guarantee. He immediately went to other two banks, to convey that he does not need the facility, because, Bobby had issued on the same day. The Manager dealing guarantees in Barclays asked him, how BOBBY can survive, if it does, without following the norms. The customer replied that BOBBY has not relaxed the norms; it has charged the same commission and same security, which was offered to Barclays. Rather, BOBBY charged 2% commission, while, one other bank was ready to issue guarantee on 1% commission, still he preferred Bobby because of the speed.

In an another incident, a customer needed a bank guarantee for rupee one million. He had his existing loan with Barclays. The property was already mortgaged to Barclays. If the party takes a loan from Bobby, he had to pay for the stamp duty for satisfaction of charge from Barclays and fresh registration of charge from Bobby. It was additional cost. Barclays was also ready to issue him the guarantee with the same rate of guarantee commission. He wanted to shift to Bobby, because of its informal and flexible style. Vikram discussed his proposal. Guarantee was for one million rupee and the building being mortgaged was earning a monthly rent of Rs.58, 000/-. Cash margin on guarantee was 25%. Vikram calculated that the total stamp duty comes to 0.75% of the amount of Bank Guarantee and his bank's processing fee for the first year was 1%. Vikram proposed that he shall waive the processing fee for the first year and sanction an additional overdraft limit of SR400, 000/- also without processing fee. It created a value for the customer. He sanctioned the guarantee as well as overdraft facility. Bobby earned a guarantee commission of Rs.20, 000/- in a single transaction and the party came to Bobby permanently.

Chapter 8

INFORMATION SYSTEM AND FEED BACK

Points to ponder

- **Educate the customer by explaining intricacies**
- **Add value to the customer**
- **Be competitive**
- **Comparison with competitors products**
- **Get feed back**
- **Know the products in the market**
- **Know the Unique Selling Points (USPs) of your products**
- **Do not irritate the customers with many types of charges**
- **Study elasticity of demand**

Kautilya, also known as Chankya, was the author of Asthashastra (Economics) during 350-283 BC. He was considered to be a great scholar and writer of Economics and Polity. His diplomacy is known as Chankyaniti. He has explained the importance of information system. It is very crucial for a business to get information. It may be about the competitors, their products, their styles and initiatives in the past, present and future, their customers and their dissatisfaction, strength and weakness of your competitors, feedback about your own products and services from the customers. Many times, Vikram would ask the customers as to what were they getting from other bank. He would certainly try to make it better.

Initially, when Vikram started popularizing his bank's retail loans, it was very important for him to know, as to what, other banks were offering. He asked his staff to get him the information about the limit, rate of interest, margin, processing fee and security for various types of loans offered by the competitors. His staff would collect the information and prepare a comparative chart. He would identify the areas of his strengths and his competitor's weakness. While discussing with the prospective customers, he would explain the negative features of his competitor's products and the positive features of his product.

Once, a lady came to him for a loan. She was already availing a loan from Barclays Bank. He asked her to close her account with Barclays and avail loan from Bobby. She was not ready, because she had been maintaining her account since she was a student. Vikram asked her as to what was the rate of interest, being charged on her loan by her bank? She told that it was 10%. He requested to show him the statement of her loan account. She showed him the statement and he calculated the interest. It was around 20%. Bobby was charging 10% daily reducing balance, while her bank was charging flat rate for the entire period. Vikram explained the difference between daily reducing balance interest and flat rate of interest. She immediately shifted her account.

Most of the banks were charging penalty for early repayment of loans. Bobby was not charging any penalty. Barclays was granting a Personal Loan limit of Rs.100, 000/- while Bobby's limit was Rs.50, 000/-. Other banks did not require any guarantor while Bobby required two guarantors. Their unique selling point (USP) was the daily reducing interest as against Flat interest and flexibility of early repayment without any penalty. If husband and wife both were working, he would make two loans to make it Rs.100, 000/-. It added value to the customer.

Vikram always tried to get deep insight into his competitor's products and services through discussions with common customers. Compare it, with his products and use a feature of his product, which is not available in his competitor's product. Bobby was opening Savings Deposit Account with cheque book facility, called checking account and without cheque book facility, called normal savings deposit account. In both the accounts, they were paying the same interest. The only difference was the minimum balance requirement which was Rs.250/- for an account with cheque book facility and Rs.100/- for other account. He gathered, through various discussions that other banks were not paying interest on checking accounts. It became his USP, as Bobby was issuing cheque book and also paying the same interest. Other banks were paying simple interest on Fixed Deposits while Bobby was paying quarterly compounded. It made the actual yield higher with the same interest rate. Therefore, in case of fixed deposit account, he would tell the comparison of maturity value of the both the banks.

Initially, Bobby was charging a processing fee of Rs.200/- for one hundred thousand, which comes to 0.2% p.a. while other banks were charging 1%. Vikram used it as his USP. He observed that customers were unhappy with different charges. One of the customers wanted to buy forex. She was having account with other banks also. Vikram asked her the rate of commission her bank was charging to her. She revealed that her bank charged four percent commission and she was not happy. She would not buy forex from that bank in future. Bobby was charging 1% only. Sometimes, Vikram would waive even 1% and make it at par. It created value for the customer.

In this way he changed very fast to suit the customers need and add value to the customer.

Chapter 9

PROACTIVENESS PASSION AND PERSONAL TOUCH

Points to ponder

- Help the customer in need- Help in need is a help indeed
- Solve the problem of your customer
- Explore various options to solve the problem of your customer
- Honour your commitment
- Be fast in your responses
- Service style and speed of responses matters
- Practical and proactive top management boost the performance of its subordinates
- Customer must feel that you are caring for him
- Develop good relations with high profile customers
- Meet people and try to solve their problems
- Work with passion
- Ensure personal care for sensitive customers
- Social and moral values bring positive results
- Personal touch pays
- End to end solution is the key

- **Influence by positive actions**
- **Cost incurred on customer care is an investment**

Construction business in the country was dominated by Jamidar Community from Kutch Gujarat in India. They employed huge labour force from India. All these contractors were initially dealing with Bobby, but gradually shifted to other banks. When Vikram took over the charge, he was surprised as to why these people were not dealing with Bobby which was the only Indian Bank. He started meeting these people and found that each one had some incidents with the Bank Management annoying them to shift to other banks.

It was a place, where many parties, social gatherings, cocktails, etc were held. Vikram made it a point to attend all the social as well as official functions to enable him to meet as many people as possible. Every social gathering was an opportunity for him to meet and introduce to new people and invite them to his bank. Discuss their banking problems and help them to find solutions. Every businessman encounters a problem sometimes in his business and look towards his banker to resolve the problem. Sometimes the problem needs a banker to go some extra miles from the set norms, which may not be possible for his current bank. In such a situation, he will try and search for the alternate. A proactive banker can encash the situation to get a fresh customer.

One of the customers needed an urgent Letter of Credit. He was not dealing with Bobby. His Bank could not help him because; it needed credit as well as forex to take care of his need. Vikram had met him in a social function earlier and offered his bank's services. He was very annoyed with the bank, but when, he was in a problem, he thought to explore, if Vikram could help him. He discussed his problem and found that he had USD deposits with Bobby Bank in India. Vikram could finance him against the security of that deposit. Vikram asked for the details of deposits. His assistant contacted the branch in India and requested them to note their lien on the deposit. He immediately opened his Current Account with Bobby and the bank issued the Letter of Credit immediately on the same day. It was so surprising for him. He could not believe that a bank can issue Letter of Credit so fast. Though, he opened his account for opening Letter of Credit but still, he did not shift his entire operations to Bobby bank. After sometime, he again had a problem and needed an advance payment for USD20, 000/- to be sent to his supplier. He could not get help from his banker and came to Vikram after business hours. Vikram again noted lien on Indian deposit and granted him loan. His advance payment was remitted the same day, which, he never believed it could be done. Vikram had several more such encounters and the customer started thinking that no bank in the country can match the speed of response which Bobby provides. He said that my existing bank cannot match your style and speed. You deserve my entire business.

All the Construction Contractors were celebrating a Hindu Festival Deewali (Festival of lights) every year. They were arranging a cultural function. In 2007, the organizers came to Vikram with an invitation card to attend the cultural function. They had also invited a Justice of the Court of Appeal.

Vikram had an opportunity to meet the Justice for the first time. By chance, Vikram did not have his business card in his pocket on that day. Vikram assured him to send his card. He wanted to discuss certain banking issues. Next day morning, Vikram arranged to send his card to him. He called on the bank and discussed banking issues. Vikram found him an intellectual, knowledgeable and fond of reading and requested him to open his account. After some time Bobby released its History Book on 100 year of Banking. Vikram sent him a copy of the book due to his taste of reading to know more about the bank. In July 2008, the bank celebrated its Centenary and arranged a party.

Justice was also invited. It was a nicely arranged function. Vikram spoke on the occasion highlighting the achievement of his bank globally. He commended Bobby's performance and said that Vikarm was very proactive and resilient. He further stated that Vikram's P.R (Public Relations) was very good. According to him, these two factors were responsible for the change in the image of the bank. His wife opened her personal account with Bobby. She felt the difference in service. She referred many other friends and relatives for opening their accounts and made very good word of mouth publicity among high profile people.

Vikram had an opportunity to visit Mauritius in March 07 on an official visit. While coming back, he met four sisters coming from Mauritius to this country. They were residing near Bobby bank, but their accounts were with other bank. They belonged to a reputed business family of Victoria. They had with them excess Baggage, because they were visiting Mauritius for shopping purposes. All of them were elderly ladies with much older age than Vikram. As a mark of respect for the elderly people, Vikram offered them to help in carrying their luggage from the aero plane to come out and again helped them in removing their luggage from the conveyor belt. Their brother came to receive them on the airport, but their luggage could not be accommodated in their car. Vikram offered them to put some luggage in his car and helped them to carry their luggage. All this was done as a mark of respect for elderly ladies.

After few days, they opened their accounts with Bobby. Their brothers also shifted some of their big deposits from other banks. One of their brother discussed with Vikram about their forex deposits. They were not getting proper service from their UK Bank. They had several million GBP/USD/EUR deposits with Barclays London. Vikram discussed with them about their problems and the rate of interest, they were getting from Barclays. Vikram had few options like helping them to open their accounts with any one of their Mauritius, Brussels or Singapore branches. From his personal experience with these territories, Vikram found, the Brussels branch was not proactive and upto the mark in his personal judgment to take care of the big deposit of such a sensitive party. OBU Mauritius was proactive and fast in responses, but their rate of interest was not attractive. They were paying less than LIBOR. Offshore Banking Unit of Singapore was very proactive and offered better rate of interest. Vikram assured them the best of class service and the best rate of interest from their Singapore branch. He took the responsibility to personally take care of the service to be provided by Singapore branch. They agreed and transferred huge deposits to his Singapore branch. Now they started getting better rate of interest and personalized service locally.

They would come to Vikram for any service from Singapore branch and he would arrange it over phone/fax. Barclays UK sent their special representative to meet them personally at the residence of the party. He tried his best to take their deposits back, but in vain. They started coming to Vikram for discussion and advice on banking matters. They had some big deposits with other local bank. As a good will gesture, they transferred around 15-20 million rupee deposit to Vikram.

They also opened their business account. They were saying that all the Chief Executives of Bobby tried to bring their deposits to Bobby for the last 30 years, but failed. They were surprised as to how Vikram could succeed in getting their deposits transferred from other Banks. Many times, he would use telephone to take care of their service. They observed that Vikram spend international telephone call charges for providing them quick service. He would assure, end to end solution of a problem and try to get immediate response for getting the work done for them. They were very happy on their decision to shift their deposits to Bobby Singapore.

Initially, their loan portfolio was very small and they needed to increase it. Forex revenue was also weak area needing boost. One of the parties of Indian Origin was a leading businessman of the country. He owned hotel, restaurant, amusement centre, inter lotto (lottery), Super Market, construction, hospital etc. and providing employment to around 1000 people. Being a person of Indian Origin, Vikram wanted him to deal with Bobby Bank for his banking needs. He had his accounts with Bobby in the past, which had been transferred to other bank. All his accounts were inoperative with negligble balances. Vikram tried to seek appointment with him to discuss about his banking needs. Despite, sincere efforts several times, he could not get appointment for more than one and a half year. His financial staff told Vikram that Bobby would not be in a position to provide the services he needed. Once, he had a project for the construction of a building for commercial use. He came to Vikram for discussion. Vikram offered him the most suitable terms for the loan assuring him the disbursement within a very short period. He was very happy. He was in the process of taking approval from planning department. It took time and in the meantime he bought another hotel. He was in urgent need of funds to the tune of Rupee 7-8 million. He again came to Vikram for help. Hotel was already mortgaged to another bank. It could not be mortgaged before the repayment of loan taken by previous owner. Sale deed was yet to be created. This property was not available as security. Vikram discussed various options with him. He found that he had some good deposits in India. Some of the deposits were with Bobby bank and some with other banks. Vikram suggested him to transfer the deposit from other banks to Bobby. He could consider loan against the security of the deposit with Bobby bank in India. He agreed but the loan limit needed was beyond Vikram's powers. He referred the matter to his Mumbai Office. Chief Manager dealing with loans raised an objection that Reserve Bank of India does not allow loans against non resident deposit for more than rupee two million. Vikram knew that this restriction was applicable to Indian branches only, and not the foreign branches. He needed urgent disbursement of the loan. Vikram talked to DGM, International Operations, as GM was not available at that time. He refused to disburse the loan without their prior approval. It was very urgent and the party had committed the payment before a certain date. Vikram was in a fix. He wanted to help the party. It was risk free advance, but still, he was not getting a go ahead. Somehow, Vikram could contact the GM International Operations Mr. Bansal. He was a very professional and practical banker. Vikram explained him the situation and requested him to give a go ahead, so that his action would be confirmed by him later on. There was no time to seek prior sanction. Vikram had committed the disbursement before time to the party.

Vikram explained his GM that he had already committed the party. It had to be honoured in any case. General Manager immediately allowed him to go ahead. It gave him a big strength and support. Vikram disbursed the loan and wrote for confirmation of his action, which was confirmed in due course. Party was so obliged for this timely help, which he could not have got from any other bank. Now, Vikram developed good relations with this party. Contact with this party was no more a problem as in the past. Still the party had its main dealings with another bank.

After some time, Govt. of the country started privatization of its Parastatal units. Party put a bid to buy milk and juice manufacturing units. It was for Rs.23 million. Party was successful in the bid and paid Rs.2, 000,000/- in advance. It still needed to pay Rs.21 million. Now the fund position of all the banks was very tight. Treasury Bills were yielding interest @ 30%. Loan interest rates were around 18%. No bank was interested in loans. Vikram was managing his resources in such a way that his liquidity position was comfortable. He needed to increase loan portfolio as a long term strategy. He knew that the treasury bills rates of 30% may not last long and it make sense to grant loans to good borrowers.

Party again contacted him for the loan. Though, the limit was within his powers, but the single borrower/group borrower exposure cap was going out. Vikram needed to seek approval from his Mumbai Office as well as Central Bank of the country. Again, it was a time bound proposal. The party had to make payment to the Government before the specified date. Vikram immediately put up a proposal for relaxing the exposure norms from his General Manager International, as well as Central Bank of the country. It was followed up with telephone call. He was hopeful to get approval from his GM (Intl) Mr. Bansal. He talked to him personally, explaining the proposal which was otherwise within his lending powers. General Manager immediately agreed. Vikram then talked to the officer concerned with Central Bank of the country. He also informed that they will be giving permission, though, it was not yet signed. He disbursed the facility after getting the documents. It was so fast that the party could honour its commitment of payment to the Govt. Now the party realised and expressed that Bobby bank was unparallel. He advised his finance department people to shift entire business to Bobby gradually. He expressed that he could feel the difference in service style and speed of responses which matters a lot. Party told that they will reciprocate. Now Bobby was their own bank.

Chapter 10

Visualise the Future Market

Points to ponder

- **Think ahead**
- **Be the first mover**
- **Offer high rate before your competitors**
- **Understand the implications of business environment**
- **Create faith in the mind of people**

There are many players in the market. Every Player has a different style of business. Everybody has different perception and understanding of the market. If one can understand the market trend and adopt appropriate strategy well in time, he will be the most successful. The best doctor is one who can diagnose perfectly. Prescription and treatment can be administered by anybody. Therefore, the most successful business leader is one who understands the market and visualizes the future market perfectly.

IMF was studying the economic imbalances in the country. Central Bank of the country and the IMF were of the opinion that exchange rate of USD Vis a Vis rupee should be between rupees 12-14 a USD after the float of rupee on market forces. In Vikram's opinion, the exchange rate should have been minimum rupee16 a USD which would show depreciation of rupee by more than 100%. As soon as the rates were left to the market forces, most of the banks started from Rs.13/- per USD. Bobby immediately increased it to Rs.14/- and bought ample amount. There was very good demand at Rs.14.75 to Rs15/-. Bobby immediately sold and kept on squaring off its position. All the banks were allowed by Central Bank to change the card rates thrice a day. Some banks kept on increasing the rates and their buying rate increased to Rs.25/- while other banks were selling at around Rs.17-18. Public started buying from one bank @ Rs.17-18 and selling at Rs.25/- to another bank. There was a big chaos in the market.

Central Bank called bankers meeting and advised all the banks to contain the rates. Public did not have faith in the market. Scarcity of forex in the country for the last many years had created thinking in the mind of people that they must buy and hoard the currency. It may not be available after some time. Before the liberalization of the forex market, any retail buyer was allowed to buy USD400 against a travel ticket. Production of ticket was no more a requirement after liberalization. Bobby stopped asking for the ticket. Some banks were still insisting for the ticket. Initially, Bobby started selling to its customers only. Slowly, when they observed that inflow of forex has increased, they started selling to non customers also without asking for any proof. Vikram increased the buying and selling rates with ample margin of profit due to uncertain market. Other bank's customers started coming to Bobby due to hassle free sale without asking for evidence of requirement.

In view of the Central Bank meeting and directions to contain the rates, all the bankers had a meeting and decided to fix the rates of USD verses rupee @ 13. TT Buying and currency buying vis-à-vis selling rate were decided to be kept at a specified margin. Currency and TT buying of all the banks were to be kept within a range of 25-50 cents. Central Bank advised the maximum margin of profit to be kept at the rate of rupees one per USD/EUR/GBP.

Vikram said it won't work because; one rupee margin in each USD/EUR/GBP will create an opportunity of arbitrage. It needed to be kept at the international cross rates of these currencies. Next day, all the banks started at a buying rate of Rs.13 to 13.50. Decision of margin of rupee one could not work. Ultimately, all the banks decided their different selling rates keeping in view the cross rates. Rates could not stay @ Rs.13 for a long time. Within a week, rates moved to Rs.18/- per USD. Bobby made very good profit through forex trading. As long as, there was high demand, their profit margin was very high between 13 – 20%. As soon as the demand declined, Vikram reduced the margin by keeping his buying rate as the highest and selling rate at the lowest among all the banks. They started selling with a profit in the range of around one to ten cent per USD.

Apart from forex market, interest rate scenario also changed due to liberalization. Central Bank of the country, removed the specified minimum interest on deposits. Surplus balances with Central Bank were earlier yielding interest @ 5.25% which was now discontinued. A new facility of Deposit Auction Arrangement for 7 days, 14 days and 28 days were introduced to place surplus funds with Central Bank. Central Bank started selling 91 days Treasury Bills. Most of the banks were of the opinion that the deposit interest rate may go upto 12% but, they were not sure as to how long these higher rates may continue. Most of the banks were accepting deposit for 3 months at higher rate, while lower rate for more than 3 months. Vikram was of the opinion that the Govt. has decided to implement IMF package. They will have to implement it in toto. It was not possible to leave the IMF package, if the Govt. wanted help from IMF. According to the initial estimates, IMF package was to be implemented over a period of three years.

Vikram could understand that rupee was kept at a rate of Rs.5.5 per USD for many years and then increased to Rs.8. It was artificial rate. It did not have enough strength to be at that level. It was being traded in black market @ Rs.13/- per USD. Its real value cannot be stronger than that of black market rate. It was needed to mop up liquidity from the market so that there would be no money with the public to buy forex. Many people had forex deposits outside the country. They did not have any incentive to bring their forex in the country. It was a compulsion to increase rate of interest. Increased interest would motivate people to deposit local money to earn higher interest.

High interest on loans would motivate them to bring their forex in the country, convert to local currency and repay their loans and surplus money to be kept in deposits. Bobby offered highest interest on deposits for two years. Within a short period, rate of interest on Treasury Bill increased to more than 30%. Even 7 days deposit auctions started yielding @ 30% p.a. Public was allowed to invest in

Treasury Bills. Bobby increased its interest on three months deposit to 18% p.a. As soon as Vikram published in the news paper, there were many calls from other bank customers to place deposit with Bobby. In the first week of May, 2009, rate of interest on Treasury bills dropped to 17%. Their rate was 18% and Bobby got substantial deposit in the first week of May 2009. Immediately they reduced the rate to 11% and after one month they again dropped to 9% for three months. The deposit mobilized at 18%, was retained at 9% after 3 months. Small economy will have very fast impact of any variable. Vikram's thinking of rate of interest to remain high for at least two years proved wrong. Government of the country decided to reduce borrowing and the Treasury bill auctions were abruptly reduced. Though the govt had given a schedule to sell Treasury bill on weekly basis to the tune of rupee 200-300 million, which was cut to rupees 5-8 million without any notice. Government reduced the borrowing and released a liquidity of at least rupees 600 million in the market. All the banks became surplus with funds. Treasury bill rate of interest started falling with a great speed. Every week the rate will fall by 2-3%. It was unexpected and banks could not reduce their interest on deposit with the same speed. Vikram started putting funds in 365 days Treasury bill, when he saw the market going down. Upto some extent, he could hedge his risk. He learnt a lesson that in a small economy, you cannot predict as to how the market will move. Small jerk can shake the market. One should not take long term view based on the present rate.

Chapter 11
NET WORKING AND LIASONING

Points to ponder

- **Educate the customer**
- **Liaise with people taking decisions**
- **Liase with opinion makers**
- **Provide more value than competitors**
- **Help in personal banking need of Corporate customers**
- **Explain the customer, how he can benefit**
- **Keep chasing for more business**
- **Take care of customer's need**

Business is all about customer relations. Business need to manage its relations with the people who matter for taking decision. Other important categories of people were the people, who are highly placed and their word of mouth matters. These VIPs may not be beneficial directly into the business, but indirectly they play a very crucial role in forming opinion by the people, who matters for taking decision. All the Chief Executives of Corporates would directly use the services of a bank. Net working with this category of people is of utmost importance.

During the initial period of posting, Vikram paid visits to all the Chief Executives of Corporates, Parastatal units and leading business firms. He tried to be in constant touch with these people. Some of the people became very good friends. One of these friends was the Chief Executive of a Parastatal organization. Initially, Vikram tried to convince him to open account with Bobby. He made a presentation to their Staff for loans. Some of their staff availed loans from Bobby. Then Vikram had discussions with their finance team for canvassing their account. They opened their current account, but did not operate it for a long time. Vikram tried to convince their financial controller to start operating the account. He said that it was not convenient for him, because other banks had extension counter near their office and they need not to send a person to deposit their cheques on daily basis. Chief Executive had become Vikram's friend. He used to come to Vikram for his personal banking needs. After few visits, he felt the difference in service quality and speed of responses. He would discuss banking topics with Vikram and the way to utilize their surplus funds profitably.

Once, Vikram suggested him to place their surplus funds lying in current account into Fixed Deposit. He explained him that minimum current deposit balance which is always outstanding in the account can be placed. They can keep little more cash balance to take care of regular payments. Bobby was offering higher rate than other banks. He understood and liked the idea. He was surprised as to why his financial controller or his main banker did not tell him this idea. He immediately decided to place rupee two million in fixed deposits for 6 months with Bobby.

Still, it was not enough for Vikram. They were in regular need of forex. It was a weak area for Vikram. He requested Vikram, if he can help them in forex. Vikram told him that Bobby can take care of their small requests. They started sending their request to him. It resulted into operation in the account. In the meantime, forex liberalization started and Bobby's forex situation improved. They requested for some big transfers, Vikram arranged these for them.

Now their old Financial Controller had resigned and next in ladder became the Financial Controller. Their main banker was not helping them in providing forex, while forex situation of their main bank was better than that of Bobby. They shifted their entire pending forex request to Bobby and Vikram remitted all their payments. They realised that Bobby was taking care of their requirement, better than their main bank. They started sending rupee four million in their account every month. It took Vikram two years to succeed, to make them operate their account and transfer main business dealings with Bobby bank. While implementing the IMF package, a new governor had joined as the old governor of Central bank had resigned. New governor was a very nice guy and a very good friend of Vikram. He liked Vikram due to his knowledge and positive and helping attitude. Many a time in the meetings, he will listen to Vikram as he will find a value in it. Most of the staff of Central bank developed friendship with Vikram. After four year of the tenure of Vikram in that country, now it was the turn for him to come back to India. A separate farewell was arranged by the Banker's association, wherein, governor and the deputy governors were invited as guests. He was the Chairman of Bankers association at that time. Governor requested Vikram to spare some time for a separate farewell by the staff of Central Bank. Since, Vikram had developed very good friendship with the governor and the staff of Central bank, he immediately agreed. A separate dinner was arranged at a hotel. Everybody spoke very good about Vikram. Governor asked one of his Head of the department Ms Jimi Samson to offer the memento to Mr. Vikram on behalf of Central Bank. While handing over the memento, she said, Doctor, you have always been meeting with us in Indian style by shaking hands. Today you will have do as per English style. Their style of greeting was through a kiss. She will kiss Vikram and he will have to kiss her. Governor told that at least, Doctor will remember this kiss in future. It was a warm kiss and really Vikram still remember it.

Last day of working at the territory was also memorable, as, staff gave a farewell party to Vikram. It was dinner party arranged at the bank only. Entire staff enjoyed till late in the night. Dinner was arranged from a hotel which prepared Indian cuisine. They always arranged vegetarian food for Vikram, while the entire staff will take non vegetarian food. Staff was taking so much care for Vikram that even if there is some egg in some biscuits, they will tell Vikram saying please do not eat it, it is not for you, it contains egg. We have another biscuit for you. Entire staff had a nice evening. Late night, after the party was over, staff asked Vikram to come to his cabin and meet each staff separately as they wanted to hug him. He respected the feelings of the staff and each staff hugged him. Some of the staff member still reached airport in early morning to see off Mr. Vikram.

Chapter 12

Reporting of Performance

Points to ponder

- **Convince the bosses with figures**
- **Make analyses of entire data more than the usual requirement**
- **Keep constant watch on important business figures**
- **Plan everything**
- **Prepare teams for different jobs**
- **Help the senior executive in preparing for discussions**
- **Arrange for interaction of senior executive with high profile people who matter**

Performance and its reporting are equally important. A Chief Executive Officer might be performing well but the presentation and reporting of performance to higher ups or Board of Directors or the stakeholders provides actual recognition to the Chief Executive. One must be perfect in analysis of data. Comparative presentation of data in a way, to bring the actual work to light is a must. Comparison of past data with the present performance as well as budgeted figures of the past and present. Comparative analysis of peer banks and other competitors, market share in business and profit, productivity in terms of business growth, profit per employee, business per employee, return on capital return on assets, cost of funds, yield on advances, cost of deposits, cost income ratio etc. There are several parameters to be studied and analyzed for the past and present. It will also form the base for future planning.

Immediately after taking over charge of the territory, Vikram asked his Secretary to prepare a small diary to note down daily important business figures. Their different category of deposits i.e. Savings Deposit, Demand Deposits and Term Deposits with total deposit, advances, profit, investments, Central Bank balances, cash ratio requirement, local currency cash balance and foreign currency cash balance were being noted by his Secretary every morning and Vikram would keep a watch on his business. It gave him immediate signal, if any category of deposit was going down or not moving up. Advances figure would give him the light about the level of utilization of advances and the growth in advances portfolio. Profit figure will give him a light as to where his business was moving vis-à-vis his target of profit. He can decide, if, he needed to find ways to boost his profit or change pricing of any product or service. Central Bank balances would let him know his position with regard to observance of Cash Ratio with Central Bank and deployment of surplus fund in the Inter-Bank Market. How much funds were available for buying forex to earn profit from forex trading. Cash balances would let him know the idle cash lying with the bank, if it was going beyond the cash retention limit or losing interest on Central Bank account. In this way, these figures enabled him to keep a watch on business profit and fund management to ensure optimum use of resources and profit planning.

His D.O. letter to his Chairman would comprise comparative data on new accounts opened, new loan sanctioned with number and amount, movement of various category of deposits during the month with comparison of data of previous month and previous year for the same month to show year to year growth and also the data for the last two financial years ending March. It would give a clear picture to the Chairman, as to how the business of this territory was moving. Every quarter ending, reporting of data would contain a comparison of last 5 years and quarter to quarter growth as well as year to year growth.

Apart from the usual data provided in the prescribed format in an excel sheet, his Demy Official (DO) letter would contain almost all the performance parameters and ratios forming part of the bank's annual report. Comparison of data in such a way would give clear picture of the performance reflecting the business trend.

Mumbai office usually monitored the business figures in Indian Rupee term. It was affected by the devaluation of Rupee by 45%. Mr. Bansal took over the charge as General Manager International. He observed the figures in Indian Rupee term and observed that there is no growth of business in the territory. He wrote a DO letter, expressing the concerns on the performance. Actually, the performance of the territory was very good in Rupee terms. Within a period of one and a half year, the business had grown several times. Vikram's growth was 21 times higher than the average growth of the territory for the last 28 years. He presented the figures and explained that the actual growth of business and profit was excellent and more than the targeted growth in rupee term, but devaluation of local currency had effected the performance in Indian Rupee terms. After that, Mr. Bansal supported Mr. Vikram a lot in his decisions, to grow his business. Practical approach and positive attitude towards all his business decisions helped a lot and motivated him to increase the business. Within a period of thirty months, deposit increased by two and a half times, advances ten times, profit seven times, number of deposit account two and a half times and number of advances account nine times. Rating score of the territory during internal inspection increased from 71% to 91%.

A Chief Executive need to study the basis of performance parameters on which the performance was to be evaluated. Only the performance was not enough. Though the performance of his territory was excellent, but the rating of the territory could be increased from 71% to 82% only, in the first year of his working. He studied the rating of the territory for the last year and identified the gaps resulting in poor rating. Certain minor things needed attention and urgent action. There were certain scores for putting a complaint box in the branch, ultraviolet ray machine, attending of earlier inspection reports and sending their rectification certificate. Vikram focused on these petty items also and the rating increased to 91.4% in the second year and again maintained in the third and fourth year at the same level.

Visit of Executive Director

Sometimes, it is very important to call the top executives to have a feel of the working and getting direct feedback from the customers. Vikram invited his Executive Director to visit the territory. There were several issues to be discussed with the government. Invitation was accepted by the Executive Director and informed to Vikram. Vikram started planning for the visit. Vikram prepared the comparative data of the territory for the last five years. Apart from that he prepared a list of all the issues to be discussed with various authorities. A list of all the issues was prepared and classified into various categories.

Issue to be discussed with the government
Issue to be discussed with the President / Vice President
Issues to be discussed with the Finance Minister
Issues to be discussed with the Central Bank
Issues to be discussed with the High Commissioner of India
Issues which may be raised by press and media.

Vikram prepared the write up of his stand on all these issues and sent to the Executive Director well in advance along with pending issue if any at Corporate Office Mumbai. Vikram asked his secretary to fix up appointments with the President / Vice President of the country, Finance Minister, Governor of Central Bank, some other high profile people of the country and his high profile customers for special meetings and other big customers for a customer meet. A cocktail party followed by dinner was arranged and a hotel was booked well in advance. Menu for the food and drinks was also finalized in consultation of the High Commissioner of India. Matter was taken up with the protocol officer of the government and airport authority of the country to make arrangement to receive the Executive Director at the airport through VIP lounge. Staff members were allotted duties to take care of the sightseeing and other logistics. Plan for the sightseeing was also decided and the places to be visited and the time of the visit. List of snacks and cold drinks to be taken along while going for sightseeing was prepared.

The entire event was so nicely planned that the programme was appreciated by everyone. Many high profile people of the country including Vice President of the country attended the event and everybody appreciated the transformation of Bobby bank in the recent past. It was very nice and enjoyable moment for the staff and the customers. Executive Director was extremely happy with the performance and the feedback received from the public.

Chapter 13

INCREASE IN CUSTOMER BASE TO MULTIPLY BUSINESS

Points to ponder

- **Sound customer base is a must**
- **Observe the positive part of an action as well, instead of negative only**
- **More customers give scope for variety of business growth**
- **Every problem has an hidden opportunity, identify it**
- **Today's problem may be tomorrow's business growth potential**

Vikram's predecessor was not allowing opening of new accounts and the public was under the impression that Bobby was not opening any account. On his first day of reporting, a customer was requesting for opening an account which was refused. Vikram asked about the reason for not opening the account. He was told that everybody wanted to open account for getting forex. Bank had acute shortage of forex and therefore, unable to take care of the forex demand of its customers. Vikram did not say anything at that time, but, it was a very important and critical issue for him to address. In his opinion, increase in customer base was very crucial and entire business strategy would depend upon the customer base. Bank's existing customer base was very low and business growth with that level of customer base was not possible. He found that other banks were also discouraging the opening of fresh accounts.

Vikram could understand very well that forex was a problem and it was not possible for him to take care of forex demand of even existing customer. They did not have enough customer base to increase retail loan portfolio, hence, needed more customers to increase the demand of retail loans, which was very crucial. Bobby's loan portfolio was very low and needed big jump. Treasury Bills and Bonds provided very little yield and even the opportunities for deployment in Treasury bill was limited. There was no secondary market of securities. Deployment of funds was also a big challenge. Bobby did not have ATM facility. ATM could not be viable unless, they increase the number of customers to utilize the ATM optimally. As explained earlier, they decided in their staff meeting to double their customer base within one year. Vikram advised his staff about the need of increase in customer base to go for ATM facility and ample number of borrowers for retail loans. Positive factor, to justify the need of increase in customer base were more than the negative, which was only forex demand. Initially, they started advising the new customers that they may not be in a position to assist them in forex. Bobby started granting loans to new customers at a very fast speed. They devised a check list and implemented it. They started asking for a statement of account from other banks for granting loans and waived the condition of six month banking relationship with Bobby. Bank started getting very good response for opening fresh accounts through its publicity and advertisement.

In one of Vikram's meeting with the Director of Social Security Fund, she explained a problem of distribution of monthly stipend to students of Polytechnic level. Banks were not opening their accounts. They had to distribute cash. Vikram proposed them to open their account with Bobby and asked them to send a list with a cheque to the bank. They issued a circular that Bobby Bank would open their accounts and advised them to contact Bobby for opening the account. Bank got good number of accounts of young students who would be major within one year and all their future banking needs would be provided by Bobby.

Some of the people, who sold their property in forex, opened their local currency account with Bobby. While the main proceeds were in forex and it did not come to Bobby bank at that time. Slowly, as they needed some money, they started transferring their forex funds and converted to local currency. When the Govt. of the country started liberalization of the economy, local currency depreciated to more than 50% and it motivated people to convert their forex to local currency. In their Endeavour to increase their customer base, they mobilized some business accounts and their variety of banking needs multiplied their business. Increase in customer base could enable the bank to justify the viability of their ATM project. Some of the customers wanted to open their accounts with their branches overseas. While, Vikram helped them to open their accounts overseas, they started meeting him frequently for providing help in dealing with their account and ultimately they were convinced to open their local account with Bobby also. It provided a very good opportunity to mobilize variety of business through these customers.

CHAPTER 14

INVOLVEMENT

Points to ponder

- **Involve in operations to know the performance**
- **Check reporting figures**
- **Keep a watch on big figures**
- **Keep a watch on operational problems**

A Chief Executive cannot feel the pulse of business, unless, he is fully involved in the business. Strategy, planning and its execution is the main job of the CEO, but he must know the results and operational performance on the ground. As a Chief Executive of a bank, one needs to be in touch with the figures of Balance Sheet and Profit and Loss account.

Keeping in view the above aspect, Vikram made it a point that daily cash book/day book was checked by him. It helped him to feel the pulse of his business. He could monitor the cash position, Central Bank balances, foreign currency bought, sold and currency balances, NOSTRO account balances, profit and other similar figures. When he observed the foreign currency balances are increasing beyond a reasonable level, prices of forex will be reduced and realigned to discourage further purchase and encourage sale. While, low balances of foreign currency in hand would hint him to increase the rates to purchase more and sell at higher price. Similarly, NOSTRO Account transaction in different currencies would hint him about the available balances to deploy them profitably and drawing of DD and TT for the customers and funding of account in time for smooth functioning. In case, some big amounts of Fixed Deposits were made or some loan disbursements or repayments were made during a day, all these will also be reflected in the cash book. Various heads of profit and loss accounts are also monitored through this exercise.

Sometimes, Vikram would check the operations in current accounts to know the balances in the business account of various Corporates, some big withdrawals or deposits could be tracked through the mechanism. Throughout the day, many customers would be discussing their banking problems and getting solutions, helping him to get feedback and market report about the bank.

Occasionally, Vikram tried to check the statements/ returns of regulators and Head Office. In case, some wrong reporting is being done through over sight, it could be rectified by observing the statements.

Involvement in operation gives insight into the operational problems, Sometimes technical problems occur in the system and one need to find the solution. What are the weakness of the system and how it can be removed? Operational staff will point out the problems and through personal involvement; one can get insight into it. It helps in getting the problems resolved from vendors of the system and dealing with their engineers. Vikram decided to install

CC TV system in the branch to keep a watch over the entire activities. While deciding the system requirements, Vikram collected entire data on the specification of the system. Various locations to be covered by the camera were to be decided. Sometimes customer might dispute about the cash deposited or paid by the cashier. So Vikram decided to install one camera each on cash cabin. It was installed in such a way that entire cash counting was captured by the video camera. Once a cashier committed a mistake in payment of money. At the end of the day, she could know that there is a mistake. She rechecked everything. She found a customer who altered the withdrawal form after passing the form for payment. He cleverly changed the amount in words and figures by forgery. She went to Vikram requesting him to find from the CC TV clip as to how much amount has been paid to that particular customer. CC TV clip clearly showed the amount and the denomination of the notes paid to him. Two staff members visited his house to get back the money wrongly received by him. He was absent from the house and his wife refused to tell anything. After a lot of persuasion she agreed to make a call to her husband. He refused having received the payment. He was told to come to bank otherwise an FIR would be lodged against him. Ultimately he came to branch in the late evening. Vikram showed him the CC TV clip and he agreed having committed a mistake and the money was returned back.

Chapter 15

HANDLING CRITICAL ISSUES

Points to ponder

- **Study the critical issues properly**
- **Think logically and analytically**
- **Study the applicable rules and laws**
- **Seek opinions from expert**
- **Be proactive**
- **Strategize**
- **Keep record of people meeting you**
- **Every problem has an opportunity to learn and earn.**
- **Be careful in fund planning**
- **Keep reliable customer for help in need**
- **Think multiple solutions of a problem**
- **Be careful of statutory requirements**
- **Develop systems to work themselves**
- **Raise your problem at appropriate form for solution of future problems**

Consortium of five Indian Banks had financed a hotel project in the country twenty seven years ago. Bobby was the leader of the consortium. A big business group of India was also one among the promoters of the company. Actual control of the company was with an American, who was a Chartered Accountant and a very shrewd person. The project could not be completed in time. Either the project implementation was not proper or the promoter diverted funds from the project to some other companies. It took more than 10 years to complete the project. Consortium of five banks provided four doses of finance to complete the project, but it could not be completed. Ultimately, the party approached International Finance Corporation (IFC) to fund the project. IFC agreed to fund it, but put very stringent conditions, which were against the interest of the existing financiers. One of the conditions was to defer the repayment of installment and interest till the repayment of IFC loan. Another condition was that existing loan will not become due unless Current Ratio of the company was 2:1. Promoters had several companies and therefore, a very complex structure of transactions was created to avoid repayment to Banks. IFC disbursed part of the amount, but cancelled the facility due to the default of the party. The loan was then assigned to the Govt. of the country and ultimately, Govt. assigned all the rights to a company owned by the same promoter. In this way, all the rights of IFC were given to the promoters. Promoters disbursed additional amount as loan with the priority right of IFC. It was a big hotel of more than 200 rooms. Hotel was doing well and the party was repaying its own debts instead if repaying the banks. Consortium of banks filed a suit in the past, but, lost the case due to a clause in the deferment agreement. Ultimately, bank lost hope and transferred the outstanding to PWO (Prudentially Written Off) account to avoid keeping of capital against the exposure as the recovery of dues may take several years to enforce the security. Several compromise proposals were moved by the promoters, but none of these materialized as the offers of compromise were too small to be accepted by the bankers. Promoter of the hotel was very clever. He was under the impression that consortium of banks will agree to a compromise at a through away price, as, it had lost the legal suit.

Vikram studied the file in Mumbai office, before reporting to the territory. Now, the original promoter had died and his son was looking after the hotel. It was a big challenge for Vikram to resolve the problem and recover the bank dues. He visited the hotel and met the party on his second day of reporting. It was a very busy hotel and there were many guests in the hotel. He thought that it seemed to be doing well, but why the party did not repay the debt. It was only an introductory visit. Vikram started contacting the party frequently and tried to convince them to repay the bank dues. Total dues with interest by now had become more than USD 100 million. They explained that it was not possible for them to repay the entire dues, even if they sell the entire hotel. Vikram was ready for some sacrifice and persuaded them to find a buyer of the hotel. They were not agreeable. Hotel needed some renovation ranging from USD 5 million to 30 million according to the renovation plan. They wanted a partner, who can invest for renovation of the hotel and have a share of less than 50% so that they can have control over the company. It was not possible, because any investor putting huge money to the tune of USD25-30 million would like to have a control in his hand. Vikram tried to bring several investors but the proposal could not materialize due to the lack of flexibility on the part of the promoters.

Vikram was taking up the issue with the Govt. of the country as well as Central Bank of the country to help the bank recover its dues. He requested the Govt. through Central Bank of the country to put the hotel into compulsory liquidation after cancellation of the licence.

In one of the meeting with the then Governor of Central Bank, the then Governor informed Vikram that he had a buyer and the bank will get a particular price to sell its debt. Vikram had managed another buyer, who was ready to pay substantially higher price. He requested the Governor to arrange a meeting with the party, so that bank can negotiate the price. In the meantime, he referred the matter to Booby's Head Office and the Board approved the proposal to settle the compromise at a particular price subject to getting a written offer from the party. Vikram contacted the Governor again and asked about the written offer, he refused it.

In the meantime, Vikram informed the promoter party that the Govt. has decided to take over the hotel and he will lose everything unless, he agreed to sell the property as proposed by the bank. Vikram mobilized a buyer through some valued customer, the price was negotiated. Promoter party also agreed at a particular price and the bank agreed to release the charge and settle the dues. Governor of Central Bank wanted the hotel to be sold to some other specific party and requested Vikram to fix up a meeting with Booby's Chairman at Mumbai. Vikram talked to his General Manager International Operations that the Governor of Central Bank wanted a meeting with Bobby's Chairman to discuss the issue of Hotel. He further requested him to make stay arrangements and other logistics for him. He made arrangement for stay and deputed an officer to receive him on the airport. All hospitalities were offered by the bank at Mumbai, but the deal could not be through. He came back from the meeting.

Vikram told him that he has found a buyer and shortly bank will arrange to sell the property. He further requested him to arrange Government permission for the foreign buyer. Governor refused, saying that he wants the deal to be transparent. He further told that the Government had already decided to appoint M/S Ernest and Young as the liquidator. Earlier proposed buyer had already got the preliminary permission and final permission was awaited from the Govt. Immediately, a petition was filed by the Government to liquidate the company. Bobby's deal was cancelled as the Government refused final permission stating that the liquidation petition has been filed.

Court appointed Mr Young as the provisional liquidator. Notice was published in local news papers to sell the property. Notice did not mention any currency for selling the property. In one of the meeting with the representative of the buyer, one year back, Vikram had a hint that they will manage to buy the property in local currency rupee by paying highest price. He reported that they had made all arrangements with the high level people in the Govt. Vikram was skeptical that the property may be sold for Rupee and the bank may not be in a position to recover its dues, which were in USD. Vikram advised the liquidator that the property should be sold in USD/EUR/GBP only. Bank's loan was in USD, so he should not sell the property in Rupee. He was advised to give sufficient notice to the public, so that reasonable price could be obtained. Vikram further requested him to send him a copy of the Information Memorandum to be sent to the prospective buyers. He did not agree for increase in the notice period, but agreed to stipulate the sale in USD/EUR/GBP. He also sent a copy of the Information Memorandum.

Vikram managed to send the information memorandum to all the parties, who had shown their interest to buy the property, during the last one and a half year. One of the conditions of Information Memorandum was to submit a proposed plan of investment by the buyer, which was very difficult to prepare, in such a short period. Vikram requested the liquidator to remove this condition, but he did not agree. Some of the buyers, Vikram contacted, reported that it was not possible for them to submit complete plan, within the short period. They could not put their bid.

He could mobilize only three bids. One lowest bid was put up by a party, not mobilized by Vikram. Then. Vikram requested the liquidator to open the bids in the country, so that they can monitor the process, which he refused and decided to receive and open the bids in his office overseas. Vikram requested his counterpart in that country, to depute an officer to oversee the process. Four bids were opened but the name of the bidders and the amount of bid was not disclosed by the liquidator, despite request from bank's representative.

Vikram requested the liquidator to reveal the names of bidders and the respective bid amount. After some time, he informed that the highest bid was for USD60 million. Second highest was for USD50 million, third highest was for USD25.111 million and the lowest was for US$ 25 million. Vikram requested him to accept the highest bid or alternatively ask all the four bidders to come for an open auction, if, somebody was ready to pay more than the highest bid. Liquidator did not agree to the proposal and ultimately informed him that the Govt. has approved only the lowest bidder to buy the property. Vikram objected to it, stating that lowest bidder will have to pay at least USD60 million, to match the highest bid, otherwise bank will not allow it.

Vikram was worried, in spite of a lot of home work and efforts, he could mobilize top three bids, but, these were not allowed by the Government, to buy the property. Lowest bidder then approached the liquidator to revise his bid from USD25 million to rupees 480 million presuming that it will be equal to USD60 million. Vikram requested the court not to allow sale and release Bobby's charge, unless bank get USD, the currency, in which loan was granted and charge was registered. Supreme Court allowed the liquidator to change the currency and the amount of bid. Sale of the property was allowed for rupees480 million and the charge of the bank on the property mortgaged was released by the Court. Bank helplessly kept watching the events.

Just before the hearing of the application of liquidator to change the currency and release the charge, the then Governor of the Central Bank called Vikram in his office. He asked as to what was the stand of the bank on this application. Vikram replied that bank will fight and argue against the application. Bank had financed in USD and they must get their USD back. The charge on the property shall be released by them, after they get their loan back in USD. He advised Vikram that the bank should not fight the application. He would give a letter from Central Bank to convert the local currency into USD. Vikram asked him as to why don't they allow the sale in USD and the bank get its money back. He told that the sale deed cannot be made in USD without the permission of the cabinet. Vikram requested him to immediately convert the rupee to USD on the same day. He did not agree. After the hearing, Vikram met him in a meeting and he fired Vikram left and right as to why the bank argued the case against the government.

After some time, Vikram requested the Governor to convert sale proceeds of local currency to USD. Bank did not want to fight against the government and go for appeal. Time for filing appeal was one month after getting leave to appeal. Vikram asked his attorney to apply for leave to appeal, though, they may not need it, as he did not want to fight, if conversion is done by the Central Bank. The Governor was under the impression that the time limit for appeal had expired. He refused to convert rupee to USD immediately. He proposed that conversion can be done over a period of time and the rate of conversion will be the rate prevailing on the date of conversion. Vikram requested to fix the rate applicable as on the date of sale, instead of the date of conversion. He did not agree. Bank had no option, but to go for appeal to protect its interest.

The promoter party had also filed an appeal against the order of liquidation. There were three issues in the appeal of the party.

1. Sub stratum of the company had not gone
2. It was not just and fair to liquidate the company
3. Government had no locus standi to file an application for liquidation of the company

Appeal of the party was heard by the Court of Appeal but the decision was awaited. On the date fixed for the hearing of bank's appeal, one of the Judges advised that there was no use to hear the appeal of the bank, before the decision of the appeal filed by the promoters. Ultimately, the appeal of the party was dismissed. Court of appeal will have to hear the appeal of the bank now.

In the meantime, the liquidator filed an application in Supreme Court to pass winding up order and allow him to distribute rupee, as, he could not convert rupee into USD from Central Bank as well as other banks. He charged a fee of USD 2.5 million towards liquidation fee. It was unreasonable and very high in comparison to the work done. As per the company law, the fee was to be decided by the court. Vikram asked his attorney to raise this issue in the court and request the court to decide the reasonable fee.

Ultimately, the case was concluded and the bank got reasonably good amount of recovery from the sale proceeds of the hotel and the matter was closed. Vikram was very proactive to mobilize the buyer and arrange for reasonable amount of bid. Otherwise, the hotel could have been sold at USD 25 million, while bank could manage the bid equal to USD 60 million.

Marketing Board Account

It was a big finance from one of the bank's overseas territory. Marketing Board was importing goods for the public on behalf of the government. Various LCs were being opened by them and their overseas territory will negotiate these LCs and make payment to overseas supplier. There was an acute shortage of foreign currency in the country. Government was not in a position to pay the amount in foreign currency. Therefore, bank had to arrange foreign currency loans to the government. Some of the loans were sanctioned by bank's territories under the line of credit given by the government of India. Loans sanctioned by other territories were also in default for want of foreign currency. Vikram used his liaisoning with the government to release some of the payment of installments. But problem was big and the government was unable to release the payment due to the shortage of foreign currency. In the meantime, government defaulted on some sovereign payments. It became a big issue. Lot of media coverage of default resulted in IMF package made applicable and all the payments were stopped. Government declared that it cannot pay its debts. IMF team came to the country to assist the government in its problem. Government had to implement a lot of measures as advised by the IMF. Several meetings were arranged by the government wherein, all the lenders were invited and help was sought. Paris club had a big exposure on the country. They agreed for a 50% haircut. Bobby bank had an exposure of several million USD. Government advised them that, they shall have to take a haircut in their exposure. Vikram refused to agree. There were several meetings with the legislative Committees on the issue. Vikram put up his point and convinced them that local banks operating in the country should not be asked to go for a haircut. Ultimately, it was agreed that there will be no haircut for the banks operating in the country. Now second problem arose because, the government had no foreign currency to keep the exposure duly repaid on due dates. By now, IMF had advised the country to go for economic reforms and open up the economy. Cap on the rates of the currency rates were removed. As soon as the rate was decontrolled, local currency rates increased from rupees eight for one USD to rupees eighteen for a USD. Bank had a local currency deposit as security for the foreign currency loans and immediately after economic reforms, the security remained less than 50%. Therefore, half of bank's exposure became clean. Vikram requested the government to allow the bank to convert the local currency into foreign exchange and adjust in the loan account to reduce the liability to half. Bank offered that rest of the amount of its exposure may be converted to local currency and it could be paid by the government in local currency over a reasonable time. Government hired a consultant to negotiate on their behalf. Consultant proposed that they will have to devise a very long repayment schedule between 20-50 years. Vikram had to negotiate with them for the rate of interest. It was a big exercise and several rounds of talks were arranged to finalize the acceptable rate of interest. Initially, they proposed a rate equal to the Treasury bill rate. It was not acceptable to Bobby bank. Ultimately, a rate of 1.75% over the one year Treasury bill rate was acceptable to the bank and everybody agreed. Ultimately, the issue was resolved. Had there been no consultant, bank could have agreed on a lower rate. Vikram had to take a tough stand while, he negotiates with the consultant. They will come with lot calculations on their laptop and calculate their NPV before agreeing to a rate. Bank's calculation was very simple. All the times, interest rates had relationship with the Treasury bill rates and therefore, Vikram asked them to link the rate of interest of loan to one year Treasury bill rate. One of bank's very big problem was resolved as bank's overseas territory was facing a lot of problems from their regulator on this exposure and huge provisioning would have been needed, if, it was not converted to local currency. It was a win-win for both the parties.

Cash Ratio Crisis

There were many imbalances in the economy of the country. Availability of forex was a big problem and Black Market rate of forex was approx. 150% of the official rate. In view of the economic imbalances in the country, Govt. of the country could not honour its External Debts. Out of the total Debts of USD 800 million, there was an overdue of USD300 million and the country defaulted on its redemption of Principal and interest on Bonds, due in July and October 2008. It was a big crisis and credit rating agencies downgraded the rating of the country to default grade. Govt. of the country sought the help of IMF to resolve the problem. IMF team studied the situation and proposed a package, which was implemented by the Government.

IMF advised the Central Bank of the country to squeeze the liquidity from the system, so that there is no money available with the public to buy forex. They advised the rate of forex to be decided by the market forces and Rupee was made free float. Central Bank of the country stopped deciding the rate of foreign exchange. Rate of interest on Treasury bills were increased to 30% providing incentive to public to deposit money in Treasury Bills, even by converting their forex. Loan interest rate also went up discouraging people to borrow and encourage them to repay their existing loans, resulting in reduction of liquidity in the market. Cash Reserve Ratio was increased from 5% to 13% and made applicable on forex deposit also. Central Bank stopped lending to banks even for a temporary period of one or two days. Interest rates on deposit with banks were increased from 4-5% to 12-13%. But still it was much below the Treasury Bills rate of 30% and the public was allowed to invest in Treasury Bills directly. Bank deposits started flowing to Treasury Bills.

Banks had a facility to invest in weekly deposit auctions. Bank put a bid for 70 million @ 30% to be deposited in Deposit Auction Arrangement (DAA) on 28/01/09. While calculating the amount to be invested in DAA, the supervisor omitted an amount of Rs.30 million, invested in Treasury Bills on 23/01/09. Two other parties issued cheques for payment of Rs.19 million from their current account for investing in Treasury Bills. In this way the bank became short by approx. Rs.49 million. When Vikram identified the mistake, Central Bank had already accepted the bid of Rs.70 million for DAA. He immediately contacted the Head of Banking Supervision at Central Bank, with request to reduce their bid or lend them Rs.40 million for a week to avoid the violation of Cash Ratio, as Bobby's home regulator and Head Office take any violation very seriously. She expressed her inability, stating that neither they can reduce the bid amount, nor lend money for a week or even a day.

Staff talked to several parties to get some additional deposit in current account for a week, but in vain. Bobby's staff contacted all the banks for borrowing. Three banks were already tight and regretted their inability to lend. Two banks offered to lend upto Rs.17 million only. Time was very short. Within two hours, they had to mobilize minimum around 34 million rupee. Vikram had a very good friendship with the Governor of the Central Bank. He contacted the Governor of Central Bank and requested for either temporary lending against Treasury Bills or allow reducing the bid from Rs.70 million to Rs.30 million. He said, he cannot lend but will try to reduce the bid from Rs.70 million to Rs30 million and asked Vikram to wait for his response. After a gap of one hour, the Governor regretted his inability to help. He proposed that Central Bank can buy some forex, if Bobby could sell. Vikram had left with only one option to sell forex immediately and the sale proceeds be deposited with Central Bank. But Bank's long position was only USD500, 000 which could fetch approx. Rs.8.5 million. Governor agreed to buy USD @ rupee 17 per USD. Vikram requested one of their best parties M/s VJC to sell them USD 5 lac. He did not need rupee. He could have refused, as, he had enough rupee balance in his account. But he said, no problem, he would be sending a request to sell USD500, 000/-. In this way, Vikram had a long position of USD One Million. He immediately sold USD one million to Central Bank and got Rs.17 million credit in Bobby's account. He further borrowed Rs.17 million from two banks. So, they could arrange Rs.34 million and Cash ratio violation could be avoided. Bank made a good profit in the deal. But the stress on Vikram's mind during the whole day was so high that by evening, entire body and mind were totally exhausted. It was a big lesson for him, his staff and even fellow bankers. They could convert this problem into opportunity to earn good profit, though, it was all unexpected.

It may happen sometimes

Central Bank of the country stipulated the Cash Reserve Ratio to be maintained in three currencies viz rupees, USD and EUR. Rupee currency being a local currency had a lot of variation and changes and therefore required to be monitored daily. USD and EUR were not having much variation and therefore, changes were not required too fast. Rosy was carefully monitoring the rupee balances with Central Bank to take care of Cash Ratio requirement. Suddenly some USD deposit increased and it was not noticed to increase the Cash ratio balance with Central Bank. One of the problems with Central bank guidelines was that Cash Ratio was to be maintained on the current balances. In case of any breach, it was not possible to rectify during the same week. Mr. Siva, Assistant Manager was usually preparing the return for reporting the figures for Cash Ratio. Vikram advised him to train the supervisors to create a second line of defence and groom them for higher responsibilities. While explaining the system to the supervisor, he observed that they have breached the ratio for one week. Head office of the bank and Reserve bank of India take the violations of local regulator seriously. The breach was not due to lack of funds but mistake. It was a small shortfall of USD 57000. Bank remitted a sum of USD 1, 00,000 on the same day value dating the previous week. But the Central Bank refused to accept the remittance value date. Vikram talked to the Governor and requested him to condone the mistake. Governor agreed but the bank had to pay interest on the shortfall. It was a big lesson for Vikram and his team to keep a watch on all the currency figures carefully. Vikram asked his secretary to incorporate the currency wise figures maintained in Central Bank and the requirement as per the rules. A system was developed and the secretary will write the figures in Vikram's diary along with other important business figures. Now, there cannot be default as the system was developed. Even the secretary will keep a watch on the figures and tell Vikram if the figures are going near to breach.

Vikram discussed the issue in bankers meeting without mentioning their problem. All other banker were also of the opinion that one week period was too short to manage the liquidity, so, it should be at least two weeks and that too future two weeks. Matter was discussed in the Banker meeting with Central Bank. Central Bank agreed to consider the genuine concern and changed the Cash ratio period from one week to two week. Now, previous two week average figures would be taken into account for maintaining Cash Ratio and it would be maintained during the future two weeks. Now, the fund planning was easy.

Chapter 16
Leadership Defined

Points to ponder

- Be empathic listener
- Love your people
- Learn constantly
- Keep high level of energy and energize your team
- Be empathic and think from other person's perspective
- Align your actions with the vision
- Delegate to empower people and trust them
- Be firm in determination
- Work in the right direction with devotion and dedication
- Discipline your life
- Be emotionally intelligent
- Be a role model
- Simple living and high thinking
- Develop synergy and promote shared values and vision
- Be humble while dealing with people
- Develop harmony in relationships
- Integrity is a must for people to trust

- Develop information system
- **Work with passion and promote passion among team members**
- **Have patience**
- **Personal touch in relationship add value**
- **Be proactive**
- **Execution is the most important job of a leader**

Geeta, the holy book of Hindus has explained in various texts about leaders.

"Yad yad acharti sharesthas tad tad evataro janah,
Sa yat parmanam kurute, lokas tad anuvartate"
Chapter 3, Text 21

Meaning thereby, whatever action is performed or the behavior is shown by a leader, common man will follow it. Whatever, he proves by his experience and experiment, people start pursuing the same. People do not need to experiment the same by themselves. They will believe their leader and just follow. It cast a lot of responsibility on the leader so that everything falls in place perfectly. Wrong behaviors or actions of leader may create disasters, because, people will follow his actions. Again in the same chapter, it writes as under;

"Na biddhi bhedam janyed agyanamkaram sanginam
Josyet sarv karmani vidvan yukta samacharan"
Chapter 3 text 26

Meaning thereby, great people, leaders or knowledgeable or good people should not create doubt in the minds of the subordinates working under them having lesser knowledge, rather they should do the right thing and advise their subordinates or less knowledgeable people to do the same. It means that leaders should lead by example and he should not misguide his subordinate. All his communication should be very clear without any doubt. There should not be any communication gap.

In one of the text, it explains the qualities of a warrior leader

"Saurayam tejo dhratir dakshyam yudhe chpyapalayanam
Daanam ishwar bhawaschya kshatram karam swabhawajam" Chapter 18 text 43

Which means that heroism, power, firm determination, resourcefulness courage generosity and leading are the main qualities of a leader.

Lord Krishna has also given qualities of great people.

"Abhayam sattvasamshuddhir jnan yog vyavasthiti
Danam damaschya yajaschya swadhayay tapa arjavam" Chapter 16 text 1

"Ahinsa satyam krodhas tyaga shanty apasunam
Daya bhuteshu loluptavam mardavam hir achapalam"
Chapter 16 text 2

"Tej kshma dritih shocham adroh natimanata
Bhavanti sampadam devim cha bhijatasya Bharat"
Chapter 16 text 3

Leadership Lessons-Straight from the Heart 125

It explains about the 26 qualities of supreme people;

1. Fearlessness
2. Purification of self
3. Situated in the state of acquiring knowledge
4. Charity
5. Control of mind
6. Performance of sacrifice by devotion to duty
7. Study of vedic literature, which is universally true
8. Austerity
9. Simplicity
10. Non violence
11. Truthfulness
12. Freedom from anger (anger control)
13. Renunciation
14. Tranquility (peace)
15. Aversion to fault finding
16. Kindness
17. Freedom from greed
18. Gentleness
19. Modesty / shyness
20. Determination / unwaivering mind
21. Vigor
22. Forgiveness
23. Fortitude / resilience
24. Cleanliness
25. Freedom from envy
26. No desire to expect for honour

There is a lot of literature on leadership. Everybody defines leadership in his own way. Vikram has practiced leadership throughout his carrier and therefore, he has identified the qualities on the basis of his knowledge and experience. In simple words, leadership may be defined as under.

Leadership entails imbibing of qualities like, listening empathy, energy and speed in actions, affectionately developing his people by delegating and empowering them as a role model, resourceful, systematic, simple promoting shared values among his team members with humility and high thinking, intelligent in interpretation of information as well as inter personal relations working with passion and promoting passion among his team members. Each of the ten letters of the word LEADERSHIP speaks about the quality of a leader. A brief about these qualities is given below.

L - Listeners, Learner, Lively, Love his people, Logos

E - Ethos, Empathy, Energy,

A - Action, Assertive, Affection, Align the actions with goals

D - Delegate, Decision maker, Directions, Devotion dedication, Discipline, Determination

E - Empower, Empathy Emotionally Intelligent, Execution

R - Role Model, Resourceful, Resolution of disputes, Renunciation

S – Simple, Systematic, Synergetic Style, Shared values of staff, Self Purification, Self Control, Sacrificing, Studious

H - Humility and High thinking, Harmonious, Hard working

I - Integrity, Intelligent in inter personal skills, Information system, Interpreter of information, Inclusiveness, Inspiring, invigorating

P - Passionate, Promotes passion among the team members, Patience, Personal touch, Peace, Pathos

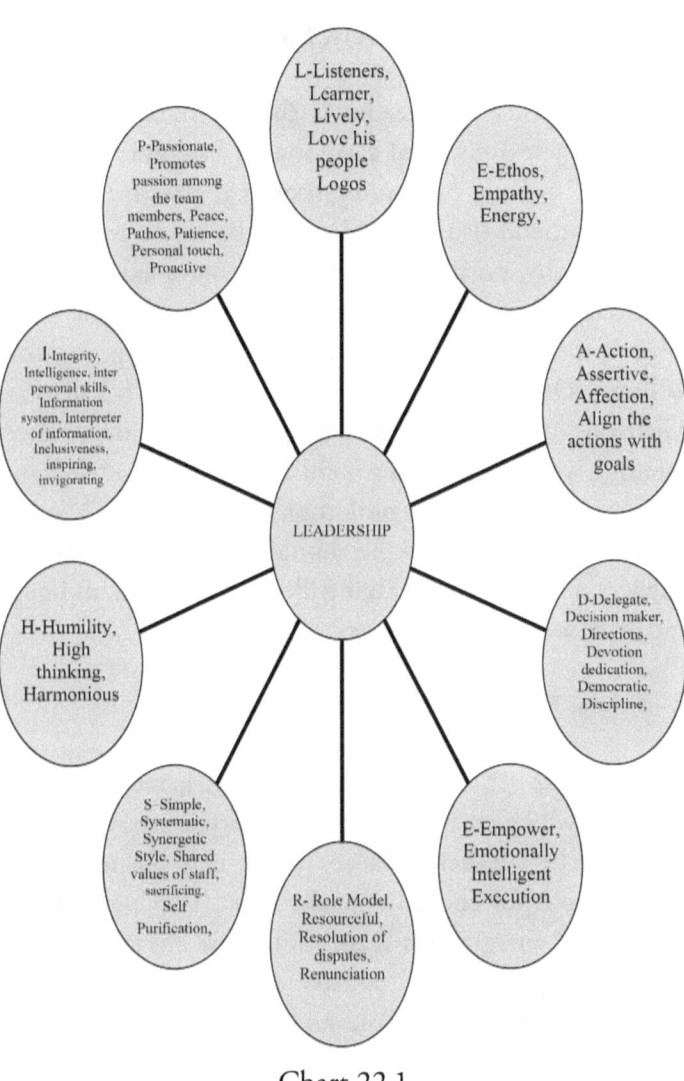

Chart 22.1

LEADERSHIP

L - Listeners, Learner, Lively, Love his people, Logos

First quality of a leader is that he must be a good listener. There are several categories of listening. Ignoring, Selective listening, pretending listening, effective listening and empathetic listening. He must be an active listener with empathy, as; lot of information comes automatically to an empathetic listener. He must understand the point of view of the teller. It should not be hearing or pretending to listen. One must have his heart and mind in listening, when, one listens. Leader is a constant learner and therefore, listening with love creates a bonding between the teller and the listener. As per the philosophy of influence, a leader must have logos, means, he should talk logic to make an impact on its followers. Talking illogical will spoil his image and after some time, followers will lose faith in him.

E - Ethos, Empathy, Energy,

Again, as per Greek philosophy of influence, E Stands for Ethos which means credibility. A person sans credibility can never be a leader, because, people may not trust him. E also stands for energy. A leader must have high level of energy and energize his team. While in Physics negative will attract positive and positive attracts negative, North Pole will attract South Pole and South Pole will attract North Pole. In human relations this rule does not apply. Law of harmonious attraction is applicable in case of human relations and interactions. As negative people will attract negative people and positive people will attract positive.

Love creates love, hatred creates hatred, smile creates smile, passion creates passion, similarly, energy creates energy, and it is contagious. Positive energy from the leader passes on to its followers and the whole team gets energized. Energy must be reflected in all the actions and interaction of the leader with the team. Once, Vikram was called as a guest in a general body meeting of a union of his bank. When, he stood up to speak and walked to the lecture stand with a swift speed and spoke to the people with a high level of energy, he got feedback that entire team felt energized by the level of energy shown by him.

A - Action, Assertive, Affection, Align the actions with goals

A stands for "Action." Vision and action are the two main components for the success of a leader. Last text of Geeta says;

"Yatra Yogeshwara Krishno, yatra partho dhanurdharah
Tatra, shrir vijayo bhutir dhruva nitir matir mama"
Chapter 18 Text 78

In the above text, Sanjaya the Secretary of King Dharatrastra tells that where there is Lord Krishna i.e. the man of vision and where, there is Parth i.e. Arjuna, the man of action, there will certainly be grandeur, victory, vibhuti ie exceptional power, this is the definite policy, in his opinion.

So, the vision and action are the two important things for a leader to succeed. No leader can succeed in the absence of these two qualities. Actions must be aligned to goals. Austerity and assertiveness are the qualities found universally in the leaders of international fame. Mahatma Gandhi practiced austerity in his life but, whatever, he wanted to achieve, he could do through his action of Satyagraha with non violence and fasting. Leaders always have love and affection with their people, resulting in trust, which is the foundation stone of all relationships.

D – Delegation, Decision maker, Directions, Devotion Dedication, Discipline, Determination

D Stands for Discipline, Decision maker, Devotion, Dedication, Determinations, Direction and Delegation. Discipline is a great virtue and first lesson in life. Self life of a leader must be disciplined and one must lead by example. If leader's own life is not disciplined, he sends wrong signals to the people and the followers may not be expected to be disciplined. Devotion to duty is the quality of great people. Duty is beauty is the message to be given by leaders. When one is dedicated to a cause, and focus his entire energy on the same, extraordinary results are bound to happen. Firm determination is the value, a leader need to observe as a role model. Lord Krishna advised to Arjuna, the great warrior in the war of Mahabharata while preaching the message of 'Geeta,' the holy book of Hinduism as under;

"Vyavasay atmika biddhirekeh kurunandan
Bahushakha hyantaschya buddhayo avyavsayinam"
Chapter 2 text 41

Resolute, focused, determined mind is only one. If a person is lacking in firm determination, his mind is divided into several branches. He cannot be focused, those who are not focused are bound to fail and cannot expect success. There is an incident. Once, Mr. Pratap Singh Cairo, a Chief Minister of an Indian State was travelling in his car during night. A hare came on the road to cross it. Driver was perceiving that hare is a very fast moving animal and it will cross the road by the time car reaches it. After seeing the lights of the car, hare became indecisive and stopped in the mid of the road. It tried to jump very late and ran over by the car. Mr. Singh asked his driver to stop the car and check what happened to the hare. Car was stopped and it was found that the Hare was dead. Mr. Singh asked his driver, why it happened. Driver could not reply. Then Mr. Singh explained that the hare became indecisive in the mid of the road and it was too late for him to jump out of the road. So delay in decisions is very fatal. Particularly for business people, speed of decisions is an important factor to succeed. Leaders need to take fast decision. Therefore, decision making and delegation are very important qualities of a leader, being a person at the top. People look towards him for a decision and empowerment through delegation of authority and accountability. Delegation enables a leader to share his burden with the team members and in the process, team members are groomed for taking higher responsibility. So, a leader need to Groom and mentor his people and empower them fast by delegating powers for creating more leaders. Lead leaders to multiply growth.

E - Empower, Empathy Emotionally Intelligent, Execution

E stands for Emotional Intelligence and Execution. Emotional quotient (EQ)or Emotional Intelligence plays a vital role in the success of a person. Research has proved that only 20% success is taken care by the IQ, while the rest 80% of the success is attributed to EQ. When one stands in the shoes of other person, he can properly realize his point of view. So, one needs to understand the other person outlook and point of view and only after that he has the right to be understood. A team leader will always seek first to understand the other person's view, which will create an atmosphere of a win-win team in all members. Execution makes the leadership complete otherwise, it remains incomplete. There may be vision, mission and all types of strategy, but, it needs execution to achieve the goals, without which it remains in papers.

R - Role Model, Resourceful, Resolution of disputes, Renunciation

R stands for role model, renunciation, resourceful. Role model is a person, whom people follow and like to become themselves as they see their leader, they try to inculcate the qualities of their role model. When it comes to his personal life, a leader must follow renunciation. Real leaders do not need much for them, they feel happy in sacrificing their comforts, but, they are resourceful. They can manage and find the recourses to achieve their goals.

S – Simple, Systematic, Synergetic Style, Shared values of staff, Self Purification,

Self Control, Sacrificing, Studious

S stands for simple, systematic synergy, shared values, self control, and self purification. Simple living and high thinking has been the motto of leaders worldwide. He must be systematic and well planned, otherwise the life becomes a mess and one cannot achieve the goals, Synergy is very important. Every team has some members with some strength and some weaknesses. Synergy will overcome and compensate the weakness of member by the strengths of another member of the team. It will improve the performance and it will be better than the performance sum total of all the members separately. It means 1+1 may be 11. 2+2 may be 5. Self control is to impose discipline on self. Leader must control his senses with his mind and wisdom. A leader with clean heart and mind is respected everywhere and it creates a trust among the team members. So, self purification is one of the qualities of a leader.

Taking a clue from "Geeta" the holy book of Hinduism, character of a person plays a very important role to be a leader. Senses of a person are so wild that they try to attract a person to various objects of attraction / attachment and this attachment creates a lust. Lust is the reason of anger, which results in complete delusion. Delusion is the reason of bewilderment of memory, causing intelligence lost, which is the reason of downfall of a person. A leader cannot afford down fall because, he will lose credibility and trust.

Reference Geeta Chapter 2 Shaloka 62-63 showing a chart as to how downfall of a person happen.

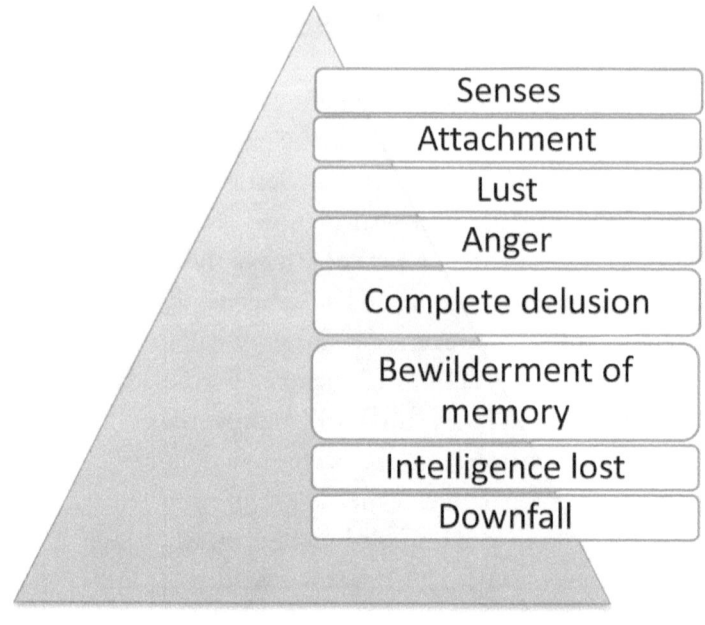

Chart 22.2

According to Geeta, Soul is supreme and next comes intelligence, mind, senses and body. Leader must listen to the voice of soul to decide the responses of his senses and body while doing his duty, which will create trust in the leadership. Reference Geeta Chapter 3 Shaloka 42 Chart No 22.3

Soul is supreme and body is the lowest

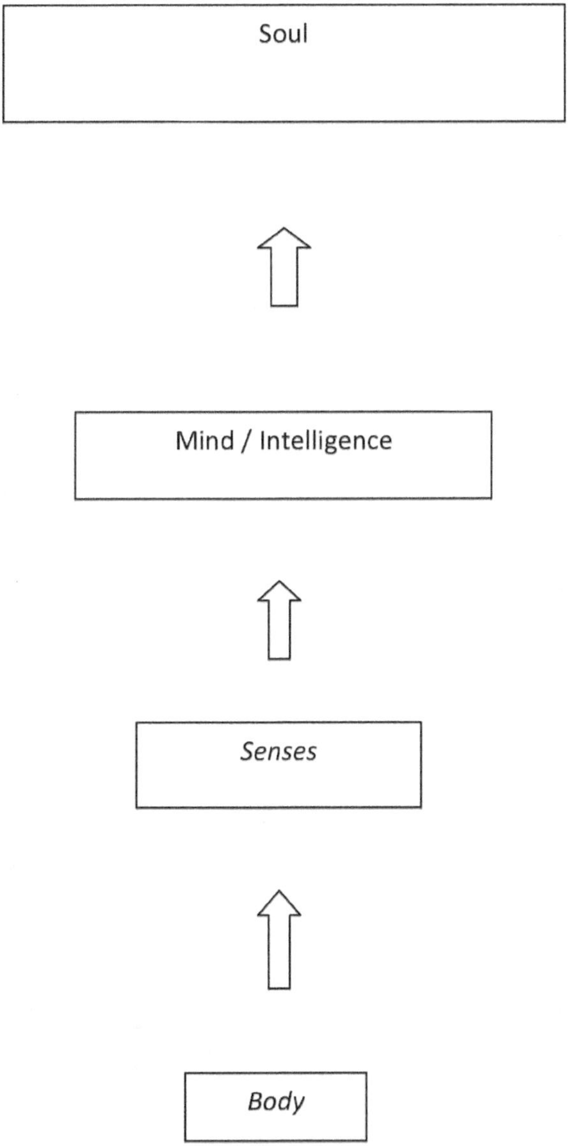

```
┌─────────────────────────────┐
│            Soul             │
└─────────────────────────────┘
              ⇧

      ┌───────────────────┐
      │ Mind / Intelligence│
      └───────────────────┘
              ⇧

         ┌──────────┐
         │  Senses  │
         └──────────┘
              ⇧

          ┌────────┐
          │  Body  │
          └────────┘
```

Chart 22.3

A leadership style must create shared values among the team to make it a cohesive team, focused on the goal with proper cooperation and coordination. Shared value or vision means that all the members of the team own the vision or value system. In case, the vision comes from the top and other members of the team are not convinced, there will be no commitment. When there is no commitment, it cannot be translated into action and there will be no synergy and accountability among the team members. Hence, the result will be unsatisfactory.

H - Humility and High thinking, Harmonious, Hard working

Eighth letter is H, which stands for humility and high thinking. Lord Krishna is a very good example of humility and high thinking or vision. He offered to be the chariot driver of Arjuna in the battle of Mahabharata. Mahatma Gandhi is also an example of humility. At many occasions, he took the responsibility of cleanliness and sanitation. He offered his services with team of volunteers as a first Aid worker during the Boer war, world war and many other occasions, which, he has mentioned in his Autobiography "My experiment with truth." As branches of a tree with fruits will always bow down, similarly the great people will always be humble. Once, the Captain of a team was called by Mr. Nelson Mandela the President of South Africa. A lady brought tea to serve to the Captain. When the lady asked the president to pour the tea into the cups, The President thanked her and advised her that he will do it himself and he himself took the kettle of the tea and poured the tea into cups. It showed the humility of a great person.

I - Integrity, Intelligent in inter personal skills, Information system, Interpreter of information, Inclusiveness, Inspiring, invigorating

Ninth letter is I, which stands for **integrity, intelligence, interpersonal skills, information system, inclusiveness and interpreter of information**. Various research, studies have proved that integrity is the most important factor for a leader. Integrity helps a leader to win the trust of his team members. When it comes to teams, interpersonal relations play a vital role for developing a cohesive team. A leader must be competent to handle interpersonal relations, because, many teams break or become dysfunctional due to poor interpersonal relations. Many times, people will say, I cannot work with Mr. X. It will spoil the synergy among the team members. A successful leader will always have an information system for smooth flow of information. All the decisions are based on some information. Information system plays a crucial role for any business. One need to know as to what is happening around, what are the strength and weaknesses of competitors, new changes happening in the line of business, which new technologies effecting the business or industry scenario are coming. New players, prices, production capacity, economy, interest rate etc are several areas a business leader need to know. When lot of information flow to a leader, its interpretation is very crucial along with the identification of information, as to, which is useful and which one is junk. Identification of talent, opportunities for building teams and business growth is an important role of a leader. Inclusiveness of all aspect of business and team with shared values of all the members of the team to take care of whole gamut of the activities to achieve the goals is very crucial.

P - Passionate, Promotes passion among the team members, Patience, Personal touch, Peace, Pathos

Tenth letter is P, which stands for **passion, personal touch, pathos, peace and patience**; everything fails in the absence of passion. Passion is said to be contagious. A passionate leader can promote passion among the team members. One can achieve anything with passion. It creates a power and strength resulting in happiness from the work, one does not get tired, despite working for long hours beyond his capacity. Personal touch of the leader in the dealings with his followers creates a bond of relationship. Where there is a personal touch, one can take more trouble due to personal relations and does not mind in going an extra mile. This extra mile brings real results to be ahead of others in the competitive scenario. When each member of the team is ready to go an extra mile, the sum total of the output will have a synergetic effect for extra ordinary results. Pathos is again empathy coming through emotional intelligence. It put a person in the shoes of the opposite person and understands from his point of view. As Stephan Covey has written in his famous book Seven habits of highly effective people that First understand and then to be understood. Most of the problems arise because people will put their point and will not try to listen to the point of the other person. Belief in peace and harmony is a must to get better results, but, having patience for the results and tolerant about the wrongs of the team members with continuous efforts to guide and motivate the team for excellent results pays. Patience is one of the ten symptoms of the religion as given hereunder;

"Dharti kshma damo asteya, shocham indriya nigraha dhi vidya satyam akrodh"

1. Patience
2. Forgiveness
3. Control of mind
4. Not to steal / no theft
5. Cleanliness of mind body and soul
6. Control over the senses
7. Wisdom / application of mind / brain
8. Education
9. Truth
10. Freedom from anger (anger control)

Conclusion

Leadership is all about imbibing the qualities mentioned above. People watch a leader and follow his actions. Parents and teachers are also leaders in the eyes of the children. Each and every person, big or small, rich or poor, good or bad has some where his responsibilities as a leader. Some may be small and other may be big. Lead with passion and energy to make an impact and leave a mark on the minds of the people near you, so that people remember you after you move away from the scene. There is a shloka in Geeta, which explains the various elements of executing a work.

"Adhisthanam tatha karta karnam ca prathakvidham
Vividhascha prathak chesta devam chaivatra panchamam"

It means that there are at least five elements to perform a work.

1. Adhisthanam means the Place of work and or the body of the person performing the act
2. Karta means the Soul or the person doing the work
3. Karnam means various instrument to be used in the work i.e. five senses called gyan indriyan (knowledge senses like eyes to see, ears to listen, nose to smell, tongue to taste and skin to touch and feel) and five karma indriyan (working senses like hands, legs, mouth, part of the body to remove waste from the body and reproduction parts of the body), mind / brain and heart etc
4. Chesta i.e. enthusiasm to do a work or the passion needed to perform, which creates energy to perform.
5. Finally the God who makes it happen through the above elements.
    Therefore, put your mind, body, heart and soul in the job, which you are doing and then leave to the God and you will be certainly successful in life. Create cohesive teams, boost energy and passion of your team to perform, celebrate and enjoy together like a family. Liaise with people and increase network so that more and more

people are connected to bring better results in the performance. Be a role model and lead by example so that other people learn by observing the conduct of the leader. Believe in action more than the words because action is louder than words. Do more speak less as the actions speak for themselves. Be proactive instead of being reactive, think ahead. Learn from the past mistake of others instead of by committing mistake yourself, however, if you commit some mistake, learn the reasons of your mistake so that you become wiser than the time, when you started the job where you failed. Keep thinking news ideas and motivate your teams to think how a particular work can be done in several ways to find the best way to do it. Welcome challenges and problems as most of the opportunities will be found wrapped in problems and challenges. Offer to help others and share the burden of colleagues without asking for it. Sense the need of others and understand the problems of other colleagues and help them solve their problems. It will create synergy among the team members. Be humble as much as possible. A tree with fruits will always bow down. Be flexible and find solutions to problems. You can either be the part of the problem or the solution, you cannot be both. Love and listen to your people to create a bond. Keep learning new things and inculcate a habit of reading books. World is a very beautiful place for the people and the leaders caring for others. Enjoy the work in your teams

www.ingramcontent.com/pod-product-compliance
Lightning Source LLC
Chambersburg PA
CBHW021951170526
45157CB00003B/946